THE END
— OF —
AMERICA?

JEFF KINLEY

THE END
— OF —
AMERICA?

HARVEST HOUSE PUBLISHERS
EUGENE, OREGON

Cover by Bryce Williamson, Eugene, Oregon

Cover photo © alexfiodorov/Bigstock; lopurice/iStock

Published in association with William K. Jensen Literary Agency, 119 Bampton Court, Eugene, Oregon 97404.

THE END OF AMERICA?

Copyright © 2017 Jeff Kinley
Published by Harvest House Publishers
Eugene, Oregon 97402
www.harvesthousepublishers.com

ISBN 978-0-7369-7115-7 (pbk.)
ISBN 978-0-7369-7116-4 (eBook)

Library of Congress Cataloging-in-Publication Data
Names: Kinley, Jeff, author.
Title: The end of America / Jeff Kinley.
Description: Eugene Oregon : Harvest House Publishers, [2017] | Includes
   bibliographical references. |
Identifiers: LCCN 2017003964 (print) | LCCN 2017022939 (ebook) | ISBN
   9780736971164 (ebook) | ISBN 9780736971157 (pbk.)
Subjects: LCSH: United States—History—Prophecies. |
   Bible—Prophecies—United States. | United States—Forecasting. | United
   States—Civilization—21st century. | End of the world. |
   Bible—Prophecies—End of the world.
Classification: LCC BS649.U6 (ebook) | LCC BS649.U6 K56 2017 (print) | DDC
   220.1/5—dc23
LC record available at https://lccn.loc.gov/2017003964

Printed in the United States of America

17 18 19 20 21 22 23 24 25 / VP-KBD / 10 9 8 7 6 5 4 3 2 1

*To all those who have supported my mission
to empower believers across America with
God's vintage truth.*

CONTENTS

INTRODUCTION

America is in trouble. Big trouble. As a nation, we are dancing on a perilous precipice, teetering on the verge of destruction. Aside from the known threats of global terror, a Middle East meltdown, a soaring national debt, and the divisive spirit that has split our nation in two, our country's very foundations are cracking beneath our feet. America is losing her *soul*. And it's only a matter of time before the bottom drops out and we find ourselves in a free fall from which there may be no recovery. It's a foreboding reality bearing down on us, and staring us right in the face.

For those of us Christians who love our country, this present state raises nagging, unanswered questions: What's really happening to our nation? What are the causes of our decline? How do we make sense of it all? Whatever happened to America the "Christian nation"? Where did we go wrong? Does the Bible say anything about our national condition? Are there Scripture passages that speak to our current situation? Can anything be done to turn us around? Or is it already too late?

There is no shortage of prophecy pundits who would sensationalize the fact that we are living in the last days of the church age.

And with these voices come a wide spectrum of interpretations and opinions regarding just where we are on the prophetic timeline, and more specifically, how the United States fits into God's apocalyptic big picture. In this book, my goal is to drown out the white noise of speculation for you by asking a simple, pointed question:

What does the Bible say?

By doing this, we can develop a clear vision of who we are as a nation, discern where we are in prophecy, and discover what, if anything, Scripture says about America's eventual demise. Along the way, we will come to those places where the biblical road ends and we can go no further. During these moments in foggy, uncharted waters, I will propose reasonable, informed scenarios regarding possible paths and outcomes. However, rather than get caught up in the confusion of the unknown, we'll spend the majority of our time looking at what we *do* know from Scripture. And rest assured, God has *plenty* to say about the end times and how the world's nations factor into it.

I trust what you encounter in this book will enlighten you. But more than merely informing you with facts, I pray it will transform you with truth. Warning: Some of what you will read will disturb you. But that's not necessarily a bad thing. For sometimes God uses the shocking truths to wake us up, instilling within us a fresh, heavenly perspective, and ultimately rousing us to action.

And that's part of the beauty of Bible prophecy. It not only reveals God's truth regarding our future, but also revives our hearts in the present. And we truly need that revival today.

It's way past time the church in America had this conversation. Time for us to talk about the uncomfortable "hard things," and to figure out where we go from here. But if you've bought this book, there's a good chance you are up for that challenge. For by facing these raw truths about prophecy and our beloved nation, you join a unique band of believers who will not only experience renewed confidence and clarity, but also respond to the call that God has issued for us in these last days.

Jeff Kinley

Is America Really in Decline?

*Look back over the past, with its changing empires that
rose and fell, and you can foresee the future too.*

—Marcus Aurelius, *Meditations*

D id you feel it?"

It was just after 7:00 a.m. last fall when I was abruptly awoken by a strange noise. An intruder was trying to break into my bedroom—or at least that's what it sounded like. The door was rattling back and forth as if someone on the other side desperately wanted in. I called out in my half-awake state, wondering if perhaps my wife had gotten up and accidentally locked herself out. The rattling grew louder and then, unexpectedly, my bed began to shake as well. Struggling to make sense of this bizarre phenomenon, I reasoned that our upstairs air conditioning unit had malfunctioned and was vibrating through the wall and floor.

Then, just like that, everything went silent. The door no longer rattled. The bed stopped shaking. The whole episode lasted only 30 seconds or so. Now fully awake, I went downstairs to look for my wife, start the coffee, and try and get to the bottom of what had just happened. Opening my laptop, I immediately found what I was looking for, in of all places, Facebook. Posts filling my feed all were asking the same, repeated question:

"Did you feel it?"

What I soon discovered was that, according to the US Geological Survey, a 5.8 magnitude earthquake had occurred moments earlier near Pawnee, Oklahoma.[1] The tremors from this moderately strong quake were felt as far away as Kansas, Texas, Illinois, Missouri, and here in Arkansas's Ozark Mountains. Several aftershocks followed. Granted, this wasn't the kind of earthquake that levels skyscrapers and devastates entire communities, prompting the dispatch of disaster relief. It didn't turn cities into rubble or create mass panic. But it *was* the kind that definitely got your attention...*and* woke you up.

Earthquakes are actually not all that uncommon. And America has suffered her share of them. But perhaps none so memorable as the quakes of 1811-12 along the New Madrid fault. This fault line, running through parts of Missouri, Tennessee, and Arkansas, also threatens many other nearby states. Between December 1811 and March 1812, a series of violent earthquakes and tremors shook this region, not far from where I live. The first of these occurred at 2:00 a.m. on December 11, 1811. A few hours later, a stronger quake erupted. Estimated to have had a magnitude of 8.6, the earthquake knocked people off their feet, destroying small towns, buckled the earth like carpet, and caused huge landslides. Hundred-foot-long fissures appeared in the countryside. Trees were snapped in half like twigs. Sulfur spewed out of the ground and massive flooding occurred due to the collapse of protective riverbanks. But the crisis wasn't over.

One month later, another earthquake hit the same area, this one so intense that it woke the president's wife, Dolly Madison, approximately 1000 miles away in Washington, DC. However, the strongest of them all happened on February 7. Experts believe it registered 8.8 on the Richter scale, making it one of the most powerful quakes in human history. This one rang church bells in Boston and crumbled brick walls in Cincinnati. Islands in the Mississippi River disappeared, and boats sank. But perhaps more amazing than all this was that this event produced a "fluvial tsunami," causing the mighty Mississippi River to *flow backward* for several hours! Witnesses say lights flashed out of the ground, thunder and explosions were heard, and black smoke filled the sky. It is also recorded that animals exhibited strange behavior leading up to this catastrophic series of events.

All told, more than 2000 earthquakes hit this region in a three-month period. The New Madrid Fault is six times larger than California's San Andreas fault zone. Experts say a similar future event even greater than the 1812 catastrophe is very possible. With no prior warning, a gargantuan quake like this would likely wipe Memphis off the map.

America's "Fault"

In what would be one of His last conversations with His disciples, Jesus Christ prophesied numerous earthquakes as a telltale sign of the end of the age and His soon return. Whether or not a cataclysmic earthquake in the United States is included in that prophecy is unknown. We only know the potential for such earthquakes *is*, in fact, a reality.

But these days, it's more than just earthquakes that are shaking and threatening our land. Millions across our country now sense that America is experiencing what can be described as "culture quakes." Far from the geophysical disruptions shaking the physical ground, these upheavals weaken and undermine the very bedrock of our nation. The tremors from these seismic strains extend across state lines, reverberating and rippling into cities, towns, and rural communities.

Yours included.

They produce deep fissures, swallowing up America's character. And they are threatening to rip us apart…from sea to shining sea.

While many good people valiantly strive to restore our country to the principles and values upon which she was founded, we still seem to be losing this war. Like rising floodwaters, evil continues to surge while virtue and decency are slandered and silenced. It feels like we're losing ground in an uphill battle. And the stakes continue to rise as the window of opportunity for victory diminishes.

Can you *feel* it?

The result of this cultural shift is that we now have a series of active "fault lines" crisscrossing the country. And with tremors being felt daily, it's only a matter of time before the "big one" hits. Odds are you're one of those who senses the hour is late, and that history's clock is close to striking midnight. Despite skeptics' objections to the contrary, Bible prophecy's *foreshocks* are proving to be true after all.

Can you *believe* it?

Do you find yourself wondering how long we have before our country collapses? Have you felt the moral ground beneath you eroding away what's left of our national character and identity? Has it become clear to you that a basic Judeo-Christian worldview, along with common-sense decency, are now becoming obsolete and unwanted? Are the words of the prophet Isaiah more specifically applicable to us now than at any time in our nation's existence?

> Woe to those who call evil good, and good evil;
> Who substitute darkness for light and light for darkness;
> Who substitute bitter for sweet, and sweet for bitter![2]

Can you *see* it?

Not long ago, my wife and I were enjoying a casual dinner out with friends, and the conversation turned to Bible prophecy. The discussion took on a more serious tone when my friend asked, "Tell us, Jeff. How close are we? And what's going to happen to America? What does the Bible actually say?"

These are questions I hear with increasing regularity these days. And it's no longer just prophecy enthusiasts who inquire about such things. Presently, there is a growing concern regarding the last days among those who previously never gave the subject much thought. This is reflected in recent research that revealed 4 out of 10 adult Americans now believe we are living in the end times as described by Bible prophecy. And among evangelicals, the numbers reach 77 percent.[3] But why? Why the sudden uptick? Why *now*?

I believe one compelling reason is because the signs of the times have simply become too obvious to ignore. Overwhelming evidence suggests we have entered the final stages of last days' prophetic fulfillment. Even the casual observer is forced to admit that we are living in an unprecedented moment in human history. Revelation unveils the fulfillment of key apocalyptic prophecies, many of which are being prepared and foreshadowed in our day. This leads many prophecy experts to believe that Revelation's day is dawning on the horizon.

But what does all this have to do with the United States? We will discuss America's future role in Bible prophecy in chapter 6, but for the time being, let's address what is happening *right now* in our country. I believe there is evidence to suggest that our current condition shows symptoms of a nation on the brink of chaos and collapse. America is not merely slipping on a downward path. We're *landsliding* toward destruction. And fast. We're in a free fall…without a parachute. And like the rest of Americans, followers of Jesus

Christ are dead center in the thick of it. We are caught in a dense, gravitational pull downward.

So what is the evidence to support the belief that our country is indeed heading toward an untimely death? Are there identifiable causes contributing to our national demise? Why are we seeing this widespread reversal and shift in thought, values, spirituality, and the law? Does God's Word have anything to say about all this? And is it too late to change? Can *anything* be done to save our country?

The Death of Nations

Years ago, while returning from a missionary venture in Central America, our plane made a brief stop to pick up passengers in the tiny country of Belize. As we made our final approach, I peered ahead through my window at an alarming sight. All along the sides of the runway were wrecked planes, both small and large. These crumpled aircraft, some privately owned and others presumably related to the area drug trade, had all crashed upon landing and simply been bulldozed off to the side to make way for oncoming traffic.

Similarly, history's runway is littered with the remnants of empires and nations that rose to prominence and power, but eventually crashed, collapsed, or were conquered. Travel back down the road of time, and you will see the wreckage of such nations. They read like a rogues' gallery of paganism:

Egypt. Assyria. Babylon. Persia. Greece. Rome.

These man-made kingdoms once ruled the known world, standing unmatched in their sovereignty. But each of them also initiated or perpetuated the oppression of God's people. What remains of these ancient kingdoms today is not much more than ruin and rubble, their greatness largely buried in history books and beneath sand.[4] And the preservation of their memory exists due to archeology, artifacts, and exhibits on display in museums across the world.

All of these mighty empires eventually met their end. This is because all attempts, whether by individuals or governments, to create or maintain civilizations while rejecting God eventually meet their own mortality.

In recent history, there have been other attempts to create world-dominating empires. Their names are as recognizable as their rulers are detestable. Lenin. Stalin. Mussolini. Khomeini. Gaddafi. Ceausescu. Castro. Hussein. And in what was clearly Satan's attempt to mimic Jesus's prophetic millennial reign, Germany's Adolf Hitler boasted that his Third Reich would last 1000 years.

It survived only 12.

Whether spending their last days in an underground command bunker like Adolf Hitler, or in a hole under a farmhouse like Saddam Hussein, all these empire builders eventually saw their end. Nations are born. They live and then they die. That's because human institutions are inherently temporary. The authors of Psalm 46 understood this transitory nature of nations when they wrote,

> The nations made an uproar, the kingdoms tottered;
> He raised his voice, the earth melted.[5]

The Hebrew word used here for "tottered" is the same word used earlier in that same psalm to describe "mountains *tumbling* into the sea." The nations men establish will one day crumble. In contrast, the city God establishes "will not be moved" (verse 5). This psalm also speaks of mountain quakes, and the earth shaking. But for those who trust in Yahweh, He is their "refuge and strength…a very present help in trouble."[6] All nations shake and tumble like mountains crashing into the sea. Only God's kingdom is established and eternal.[7]

But in spite of recounting history and remembering the crumbled ruins of past kingdoms, we Americans struggle to imagine our own country not existing in perpetuity. In other words, it's difficult for us to ponder the *end of America*. "Those were other nations," we argue. "Those empires *deserved* to die. We're not like them." We customarily celebrate America's birth on July 4, but give little thought to that time when our nation will take its place in history's graveyard. Some may argue that to contemplate America's ultimate demise is a morbid exercise, even depressing. After all, who likes to think of their own death? Isn't that a bit unnatural?

Not according to Scripture. The Bible says that contemplating our mortality is not only something God commands, it's also a very healthy idea. David wrote, "Teach us to number our days, that we may present to You a heart of wisdom" (Psalm 90:12), and

> LORD, make me to know my end, and what is the extent of my days; let me know how transient I am. Behold, You have made my days as handbreadths, and my lifetime as nothing in Your sight; surely every man at his best is a mere breath (Psalm 39:4-5).

Scripture authors, under the Holy Spirit's leadership and inspiration, compare our days on earth to a breath, a passing shadow, a morning mist, and withering grass.[8]

Our life here is finite. Limited. Temporary.

And what's true for people also applies to nations. There's nothing at all morbid or depressing about this truth. It's simply coming to terms with our mortality and reality, and positively applying wisdom in order to live a more purposeful and fulfilling life for God...while we can.

So from a biblical and historical perspective, our lives (and the country in which we live) have a relatively short life span. Like you and me, at some point in time, America will die. As we will see in the next chapter, though our country is indeed unique and exceptional, it is by no means exempt or eternal. Therefore, we must begin asking: Why, how, and when will America see her end?

Enemy at the Gates

There are many reasons a nation dies, just as there are many reasons for the death of an individual. And many ways that death can occur. The end came for one mighty nation in a single evening. The Babylonian Empire ruled southern Mesopotamia for a relatively short period, during which it conquered Jerusalem and took thousands of Jews captive, including Daniel, Shadrach, Meshach, and Abednego. Babylon's King Beltshazzar had thrown a lavish party during which he publicly mocked God's people, got wasted on wine, and praised gods of gold and silver. While all this was happening, King Cyrus of Persia and his army were systematically and stealthily digging their way into the capital city. Diverting the Euphrates River that flowed through Babylon, the Persian army gained access via the riverbed that ran under the city gates. While Beltshazzar and a thousand of his nobles partied like it was 539 BC, the enemy successfully penetrated the city's fortifications, and that night, Babylon fell. Beltshazzar was also slain that same evening.[9]

So Babylon fell in one night, whereas Rome's demise lingered like a slow disease before the empire and its "Eternal City" finally breathed its last. Rome was not "built in a day," and it didn't end that way either. Though historians propose different reasons for the eventual demise of the empire, virtually all of them agree that, over time, multiple factors were to blame for the fall of Rome. Those contributing factors include economic problems, military overexpansion, moral decadence, invasions by barbarian tribes, government corruption, and even the rise of Christianity. But these days, relatively few Americans bother to think of Babylon or Rome, and wouldn't, except for encountering them through a movie or history class.

So what about America? Are we like those ancient nations, destined to suffer similar fates? Are we really experiencing, in real time, the decline and fall of our country? Are there credible, identifiable threats to our existence? Or is this simply an alarmist's perspective? Perhaps just another case of prophetic sensationalism?

I don't think so.

I believe what we are seeing right now in our country are tangible warning signs alerting us to the decline and inevitable end of our country as a world power and gospel influence. This book will uncover the specific catalysts contributing to our downfall, but let's begin by looking at two leading causes. These are areas in which the enemy has already breached the outer gate, entered the city, and is now destroying us from within.

Declining Spirituality

In 1967, Albanian dictator Enver Hoxha declared to the world, "There is no God." With these words, he officially established atheism as law in his country. Enver's legacy would later be marked by oppression, the outlawing of private property, a government-controlled media, and the widespread violation of human rights. Today, decades from Hoxha's oppression, religion is allowed in Albania. Nevertheless, Albanians continue to suffer under the vestiges of that still-strong communistic regime.

Our government has yet to *officially* ban God and Christianity from the country. However, many of our nation's leaders have sought to limit, and in some cases, eradicate completely the traditional biblical influence and spiritual fingerprint that once marked us as a nation. Both philosophically and practically, this fundamental transformation of America is being propagated and played out in the halls of government, colleges and universities, political parties, the court system, public schools, and local communities. We have now become a society that is saturated in secularism. Those who believe in God (as defined by Scripture) are aging, and the next generation of Americans are becoming increasingly unconvinced regarding the realities of God, Jesus, sin, salvation, and the trustworthiness of the Bible.

In a 2015 study of unchurched people, the Barna Research Group found that 25 percent of today's unchurched adults are either atheistic or agnostic (Barna refers to this collective group as "skeptics"). About one-third of them have never once attended a church service. Further, this group of skeptics was found, on average, to be younger, more educated, mostly women, racially diverse, and regionally dispersed around the country.[10]

In other words, the next generation is more "gospel resistant," especially among Millennials. They simply are not buying into their parents' and grandparents' faith.

But spirituality is also taking a hit among professed churchgoers. Less than half of Americans now attend church of any kind, and for those who do, it occurs infrequently. When asked, "What, if anything, helps Americans grow in their faith?", *church* didn't even make the top-ten list! How ironic that the very institution birthed to foster and nurture spirituality and faith is having little influence in helping people grow in their relationship with God.

That may not accurately describe your particular church, but it does accurately represent a cross-section of America. Barna also found that 59 percent of Millennials who grew up in church have dropped out at some point. And finally, for all age groups, he discovered that among the reasons people don't attend church is because they either "find God elsewhere" (40 percent) or say that church "isn't relevant to me personally" (35 percent).

Further evidence of our spiritual decline is that, according to the Pew Research Center, the United States, as a whole, is becoming less religious and more secular. There are now more religiously unaffiliated Americans (23 percent) than Catholics (21 percent) and mainline Protestants (15 percent). About 1 in 4 Americans identify themselves as *evangelical* Protestants, though evidence shows that number is also on the decline.[11]

Bottom line: As a nation, we are thinking less and less about God. We are God-less. And the fallout from this fact is eroding our foundations. From a purely human perspective, you could attribute this declining spirituality to a combination of secular and atheistic voices advancing an anti-God agenda, along with Christians' failure to impact and infiltrate their communities. Many professing believers and their families seek refuge from the world and its influences by withdrawing from secular society, choosing instead to spin a cocoon of Christian comfort in their own "safe space" environment. This leaning toward isolationism is one reason we feel progressively marginalized in the marketplace and public life.

Other Christians immerse themselves into culture with no intention or skills on how to penetrate the darkness or make a real difference for God or good in their world. Some simply live decent, upright lives in hopes that others will observe them and want what they have. But some also blend in completely, adopting worldly philosophies, values, and practices. Either way, ultimately, no impact for Christ is made. And the country continues its plummet into godlessness.

America is dying spiritually.

But she is also…

Decaying Morally

Perhaps nowhere is America's decline more blatantly obvious than in the area of moral values and standards. What is openly practiced today would cause our parents' generation to blush in shame. But today there is no blushing, and there is no shame.

In June of 2015, the United States Supreme Court handed down a landmark decision, proclaiming that same-sex couples had a "civil right" to legally marry. As expected, gay rights activists and homosexuals celebrated nationwide, flooding community courthouses where men married other men and women married women. Then-president Barack Obama joined in the celebration as well, lighting up the White House façade so that it depicted a giant gay pride flag.[12] With this historic, unprecedented decision, what the Bible refers to as an "abomination" was officially made the law of the land.[13] What was once commonly understood to be unnatural and deserving of divine wrath is now widely accepted as a "constitutional right" all across this country.[14]

And with the legalization of homosexual marriage comes additional fringe benefits and rights, including tax and health benefits. Naturally, this Pandora's box of what the Bible defines as immorality, spearheaded by America's highest court, also opens the door for other kinds of immorality to be legalized—such as polyamorous unions (group marriages), men with boys (pedophilia), and even incestuous relationships.[15]

After all, "Love is love," right?

And according to homosexual advocates, government sanctioning of such aberrant unions are "not going to be as far in the future as people think."[16] NAMBLA (North American Man Boy Love Association) is seeking to make this a reality as they fight what they call the "end of oppression of men and boys who have mutually consensual relationships."[17] The ACLU has now joined them in this fight.[18] There is also a women's version of the NAMBLA organization as well, who celebrate sex between adult women and young girls.

But simply using words like *love*, *consensual*, and *rights* cannot alter the unchanging, universal moral standard as outlined in Scripture and encoded within humanity's conscience. More about this in chapter 4.

This, of course, is *not* to say that every practicing homosexual supports a pedophilic or incestuous gay agenda. It also does not imply that those who struggle with homosexual sin, gender confusion, or lustful urges are party to such radical elements of this movement. Apart from their homosexuality, many gay people lead otherwise exemplary lives. But the argument remains: If there is no God to whom we are accountable, and there is no objective, absolute standard by which to determine what is morally right or wrong, then there cannot logically be anything whatsoever "wrong" with a sexual union between a man and man, a woman and a woman, a man and a boy, a woman and a young girl, a mother with son or daughter, or a father with a son or daughter. There is no conceivable way to legitimately support an argument against such wicked pursuits without a divine, unchanging moral standard.

However, our government, its courts, and the courts of popular opinion have solved this conundrum for us. With their rulings and reasonings, they have effectively proclaimed that there is no God. And the Book Christians claim He wrote is officially unreliable and irrelevant to our modern world.

We've also seen in recent years a rise of *transgenderism,* or people of one gender transitioning to another. Though this is logically unsupportable and medically impossible to achieve (a person's DNA remains the same from conception to death), their mental perspective and self-perception *can* change as a result of one's gender confusion. Their bodies can also be modified and altered to reflect that preferred perception through surgery and other means.

When former Olympian decathlete Bruce Jenner embraced what he felt was his emerging identity to "become a woman," media outlets fell all over themselves praising and celebrating the 65-year-old man's decision. They also exploited him. ESPN applauded and honored him with the Arthur Ashe Courage Award. Six months after his "coming out," *Glamour* magazine crowned him Woman of the Year. Oh, the irony of awarding a *man* the Woman of the Year award, something at which true feminists should have been outraged. The jury is still out on how Jenner will navigate his chosen path, but if he is anything like many other transgenders, his is a decision that will likely lead him into even more confusion and depression, for research shows that 41 percent of transgenders have attempted suicide.[19]

But transgenderism is only a part of many other strains of the current epidemic of gender confusion, including *gender fluid*, or the bizarre belief that a person's identity can change over time from male to female or to a combination of both. Under the misnamed banner of equality, this twisted thinking has infected colleges and universities across the country, most of which now recognize six or more gender identity choices and sexual orientations. This is done so the schools can know how to properly address these individuals and determine what dorm he/she/etc. should be assigned to. The male or female check-boxes on college applications have now been replaced with male, female, trans male/trans man, trans female/trans woman, gender queer, gender nonconforming, or some other identity, which is a sort of fill-in-the-blank option where you can actually write in your own gender/sexual identity.[20] Following suit, ABC News has provided a list of 58 "gender options" now available to Facebook users.[21]

So how have Americans responded to this gender identity explosion? Transgenderism and gender fluidity are now widely accepted, and those who dare to stand against them, question them, argue with them, criticize them, or simply disagree with them are instantly branded with an identity of their own—namely *homophobic, bigot,* or some other word connoting a hateful, repressive, deplorable human being. There is even a concerted effort by the "gender identity police" to force heterosexuals to use "proper" gender-inclusive pronouns when referring to individuals who identify as the opposite of their birth gender or as a gender-fluid person. He/she are replaced with "zie, sie, ey, ve, tay, e."[22]

Mayor Bill de Blasio of New York City threatened business people who fail to address customers by their preferred gender (*ze* or *zir*) with violation of the law and fines up to $250,000.[23] We have truly passed through a portal to an alternate reality here.

I realize some of this may sound fantastical, unrealistic, and even difficult to imagine. But just a few years ago so did the idea of homosexual marriage becoming the law of the land. With a simple swipe of a pen, the United States Supreme Court laid an axe to the tree of morality and marriage, an institution planted by God that had remained unchallenged for thousands of years.

The impact of this decision on American society is obvious. Redefining the very idea and institution of marriage and family— as established in the Bible—fundamentally disables a civilization's GPS, leaving it to wander aimlessly. We have become a nation held hostage by whatever depraved urges and lusts our hearts can imagine.

The family is *the* cornerstone of human civilization, and the unifying fabric of any nation. Husbands, wives, fathers, mothers, children…*family*. *This* is what naturally propagates humanity and creates stable cultures. It has been the most basic institution linking humanity from generation to generation since the beginning of creation and time. Created, designed, and defined by *God*, not human courts or prevailing opinion.

Tragically, today's families are suffering, as fewer than half of American children (46 percent) under the age of 18 are living with

2 married, heterosexual parents in their first marriage.[24] This is a marked change from 1960, when that statistic stood at 73 percent. Most couples no longer marry young, start a family, and stay married for life. Now, more Americans are putting off marriage, and even rejecting the very idea of it. Living together with a "partner" has replaced traditional marriage for many. The result is that 41 percent of America's children are now born outside of marriage, compared to just 5 percent in 1960.

But when you exclude God and the Bible from a country's laws and values, this is what happens. It's another crack in the foundation of a nation, and more evidence of our decline.

America is decaying morally.

Common sense and conscience are also eroding, as we are literally celebrating sin in the streets. From gay pride rallies, misguided mass gender protests, gang violence and looting, America is losing her mind as she embraces false narratives as truth and "fake news" as reality.

Our money still declares "In God We Trust," but our actions argue to the contrary. A corrupted government and a morally bankrupt population have joined together in removing much of God, His Bible, and His values from our culture. We vehemently deny that the Creator created the world, replacing Him with a preposterous, undocumented theory of origins that is force-fed to students in the classroom. The removal of prayer from schools in 1963 was merely emblematic of a greater strategy to devalue God Himself and His role in national life.[25]

As a result, the Judeo-Christian God is now considered passé, out of date, and unnecessary. Like an expired can of vegetables, our country's Christian values and morals are good for nothing except to be thrown in the trash. It's a new day in America, and there is no room for a faith that won't allow us to do whatever we want. This is how the New Freedom is defined.

The ultimate answer, of course, is not for us to pass opposing laws forcing prayer back into schools or to introduce bills requiring that the Ten Commandments be erected in every town square. That would miss the point completely. Things have gone way beyond merely an *Us vs. Them* control for public policy or legal power. And it's not an issue of "forcing our religion" on others. It's more a matter of simply restoring common moral sense and sanity to our nation. If the basic moral code upon which virtually all the world's civilized nations are founded (don't murder, steal, lie, commit adultery) happens to align with Christianity, that does not mean the state is "establishing a religion." But it *does* mean that our nation once recognized where that moral code originated from. Sadly, we no longer do. God's standards have been replaced by the opinions, preferences, and demands of depraved thinking and political correctness.

Even Russian president Vladimir Putin has stated that America has moved away from her Christian roots and is now on a "path to degradation."[26]

Like the law of gravity, God simply *is*. We didn't make up the law of gravity. Instead, we discovered it and found ways to temporarily suspend it for our benefit and enjoyment (e.g., flying). You can deny gravity's existence if you so choose. And you can act on that denial, even attempting to *defy* gravity's force. But eventually you must succumb to its power and return to solid ground. You can jump from the roof of a skyscraper and publicly whine and scream about your denial of gravity throughout your short descent. But gravity will have the last word, catching up with you and convincing you of its reality and power.

So it is with God. The nation that denies and defies Him will ultimately collide with His reality and suffer the impact of that collision.

There is no escape from gravity. Even in outer space, you cannot avoid it. It is a force whose long, strong arms reach to the ends of the universe. And the One who created the law and force of gravity is greater than the sum total of it. God's moral laws and the consequences for breaking them are inevitably inescapable.

Because of our spiritual and moral deterioration, we have become a nation filled with self-absorbed people marked by incessant consumption, obsession with entertainment, and driven by flesh-fueled lusts. So-called "rights" have replaced personal responsibility. Moral relativism now rules the land, spreading like a demonic virus all the way to the highest offices in government. We are officially a post-Christian society. In addition, economic peril looms around the corner, with unprecedented national debt and out-of-control spending by a bloated government that is endangering our standard of living.

Experts warn that these are among the glaring symptoms of a catastrophic system failure.

The Grave Digger

Our country is racing down a path that leads to destruction. Of course, as biblically informed Christians, we recognize the source of this godless agenda and assault on decency. At the epicenter of this seismic shift in our country is Satan himself. He, according to Jesus, is a "liar and the father of lies."[27] He also called Satan "the ruler of this world."[28] Scripture further tells us that "the whole world lies in the power of the evil one."[29] The apostle Paul recognized the devil as "the god of this *world*" (Greek, *aionos* = "age").[30] He is "the prince of the power of the air," a force of "darkness" and "wickedness."[31]

Satan and his demons are *in the world*, actively destroying and dismantling all that is holy, good, and decent. And they accomplish their mission through cleverly devised, deceptive strategies and schemes.[32] Their sinister plan has a trifold objective: (1) To exact vengeance and hatred against the one who expelled them from heaven; (2) to deceive, denigrate, and destroy the crowning achievement of God's creation, those who bear the image of God; and (3) to prepare the world for the man of his choosing, whom Scripture says is "coming…in accord with the activity of Satan, with all power and signs and false wonders, and with all the deception of wickedness for those who perish, because they did not receive the love of the truth so as to be saved" (2 Thessalonians 2:9-10).

Presently, Satan is lying and deceiving the nations concerning the existence of God, the nature of man, the reliability of the Bible, heaven and hell, death, and the meaning of life itself. But every proposition he peddles is a deception and an illusion. His marketing mantra is "follow your heart"—a poisonous lie wrapped in a thin layer of self-fulfillment. A calling card of the devil is to lure you in with pleasurable poison and lies until you eventually beg for it. It is simply not his nature or capacity to prosper mankind for good, but only to pervert him for evil.

According to Scripture, a day is coming when this great deceiver will be bound and prevented from deceiving the nations any longer.[33] Despite what some may believe, he is not presently "bound" by the emotional, incantational prayers of well-meaning Christians. He is alive and well on planet earth. His stock is soaring. And he is selling his sinful shares at bargain prices, promising huge returns. Yes, this is *his* hour. He is targeting human identity ("Did I evolve or am I created in the image of God?"), gender ("Am I really a man, or could I be a woman?"), sexuality ("If I desire it, then why shouldn't I do it?"), and the family ("Why can't I marry another man if I want to?"). Of course, Satan's preoccupation with sexual deviance isn't limited to those who practice homosexuality. There are significantly more heterosexuals who are tempted by their own desires and fall into sexual immorality. A multibillion-dollar porn industry, though only the tip of this immoral iceberg, certainly demonstrates this truth.

Obviously, those who deny the existence of God will also deny the reality of Satan. But it's a dual-denial leading to a double-deception. In the end, every person will come to understand it was all just another big lie. Satan set the bait, and predictably, humanity bought it, bit into it, and was hooked. Time and Bible prophecy will prove that God is real and that His Word is true. But for many, that will be truth realized too late.

These are some of the national warning signs of a fatal illness. They are the tremors indicating an impending, and perhaps unavoidable, spiritual seismic event. America's downfall has been a long time coming. A gradual bleeding out of its most vital resources. In cooperation with humanity's adversary, we have helped to dig our own grave using the shovel of independence from God. And we have etched our own tombstone epitaph with the chisel of human pride.

But just how bad will things get before America can no longer stand due to the seismic shifting beneath her foundation? Will we simply continue in a downward spiral, or will there be some great revival that saves us in our final hour? Will we receive some measure of dying grace? Or will we reap the wrath that is deserved for what we have so willfully sown these past decades? Or could something else unexpected occur?

With the end of America, history is repeating itself, just as it has done many times before with other nations. Only this time, unlike all the others, it will signal and coincide with the end of days.

Understanding the Times

As Christians, we must respond to what is happening in our country. But we must do more than simply react. We must *discern*.

We cannot merely look at the state of our nation and world and scratch our heads, wondering what it all means and what to do about it, if anything. Instead, we must look to God's authoritative Word for our wisdom and game plan. And that's where the prophetic scriptures help us.

A significant percentage of Americans believe we are approaching a biblical end-times scenario. Even so, many Christians remain uninformed about what the Bible actually teaches regarding the last days. The average Christian's working knowledge about prophecy typically involves a rudimentary understanding of Jesus's return combined with prophetic tidbits and a patchwork vision of future world events. The primary reason for this "future fog" is that most pastors simply do not preach and teach Bible prophecy. But why? I believe this absence of prophecy in the pulpit is due to a variety of reasons. Here are my Top 10:

1. The pastor doesn't feel qualified to teach on the subject.

2. Preaching on prophecy requires hard work and much study. Some pastors may get by more on personality than having diligently studied the Word. Some pastors busy themselves with the "business of the church"— meetings, leadership duties, and church activities, leaving little time to do what God has called them to do—*preach the Word.*

3. Prophecy is sometimes viewed as controversial, sensational, and for some, even frightening or offensive. There are enough obstacles pastors face with their congregations without creating more distance between the pulpit and the pew.

4. There are divergent views on eschatology (the study

of the end times) within the body of Christ. As such, prophecy is often seen as a divisive topic, and therefore avoided.

5. To be too dogmatic or confident regarding prophetic interpretation can come off as prideful, or even cult-like at times.

6. To talk about the end times requires talking about God's wrath, and some pastors don't want to be viewed as a "prophet of doom." Negativity tends to *emptying* seats, not filling them.

7. No one *really* knows the future, so why dwell on it?

8. Many pastors and denominations do not believe in a literal, prophetic fulfillment of Scripture. Rather, they take a "spiritual" or symbolic approach when interpreting books like Daniel or Revelation.

9. There are so many more *relevant* things to preach on (marriage, handling stress, family issues, parenting, personal problems, positive attitudes, etc.).

10. Perhaps for some, they fear that if members think the world will end soon, they will stop giving financially.

While we may sympathize with some of these reasons, are any of them valid enough to avoid preaching what makes up about 27 percent of the Bible?[34]

There are some voices today claiming America is "just fine." They say we're actually *progressing*, making great strides toward tolerance, love, and equality. They say it's actually the *Christians* and those with conservative values who are the real problem. The church is what stands in the way of progress toward the betterment of our country and mankind. They allege the United States never really was a "Christian nation," and that our foundations are solidly secular. Could they be right about this? Is it possible that what Christians have long believed about America's biblical beginnings is merely embellished history?

Let's find out.

How Firm a Foundation

*It is religion and morality alone which can establish
the principles upon which freedom can securely stand.*[1]

—John Adams, 2nd president of the United States

O n December 29, 1801, a strange shipment arrived in Washington, DC. Bound for the White House, it was a gift especially made for then-president Thomas Jefferson. This particular parcel had been carried by sleigh and boat for 3 weeks and across nearly 500 miles, attracting large crowds along the way. The inspiration for this odd offering had begun earlier that summer, when John Leland, a minister from the farming community of Cheshire, Massachusetts, recruited the ladies of his congregation to handcraft a giant block of cheese. Yes, *cheese*. Measuring nearly five feet in diameter, a foot thick, and weighing 1230 pounds, the "Mammoth Cheese" reportedly required the milk of 900 cows. Engraved on the side of the colossal slab of cheese were the words, "Rebellion to tyrants is obedience to God."

The cheese was officially presented to America's third president on New Year's Day, 1802. In a letter to Jefferson, Cheshire townsfolk stated that the unique gift "was produced by the personal labor of freeborn farmers with the voluntary and cheerful aid of their wives and daughters, without the assistance of a single slave."[2] Reverend Leland had conceived of the gift as a way to thank Jefferson for his support of religious liberty in America. The cheese lasted for more than a year.

The debate over the relationship between government and religion in America has resurfaced many times in our nation's short history. Jefferson himself was no stranger to the controversy, as during his campaign for president he was accused of being an atheist. This prompted some citizens to bury their Bibles out of fear he would confiscate them. Though a regular church attender, Jefferson was actually a Deist, unapologetically dismissing the divinity of Jesus Christ while simultaneously admiring some of His teachings.

His general approach to matters of faith is characterized in a letter to his nephew, in which he wrote, "Question with boldness even the existence of a god; because, if there be one, he must more approve the homage of reason, than that of blindfolded fear."[3]

So Reverend Leland and President Jefferson clearly held opposing views on God. And yet the two managed to find common ground, merging together at the intersection of religious liberty and freedom. If nothing else, that curious gift of cheese illustrates the awkwardness that often characterizes the relationship that exists between the government and our faith.

Even so, history portrays that the church has experienced what might be called a "kindred spirit" with the kind of government established by our founding fathers. After all, it was an oppressive, tyrannical English government from which America's early settlers had originally fled. Because of this, they sought a society that would complement and support their Christian way of life, not suppress or subvert it.

Which brings us to a challenge. When it comes to telling the story of America, there are no shortages of perspectives and camera angles. That's because the recounting of history can be a curious thing, and subject to voluminous and contradicting interpretations leading to confusion. At the same time, the study of this story can also be a critical tool that helps guide us in the present. How we view the past considerably affects how we see life today, contributing toward a balanced and accurate perspective on reality. But there nevertheless remain inherent obstacles in finding the truth about America's past.

Winston Churchill is credited with having said, "History is written by the victors," meaning whoever comes out on top gets to tell the "official" story, since the other guy is either no longer in power or *dead*. Churchill was mostly right about that. However, had the great English statesman lived in our day, he might have worded it, "History is *re*written by those who *view* themselves as the victors." A sad commentary on our time, as unfortunately, we live in an age where personal opinions, strong biases, and even *feelings* often take precedence over fact and an objective historical record.

Some would even argue that there is no such thing as an unbiased account of history. And there is certainly some truth in that. Half-truths, carefully edited accounts, and misconstrued quotes muddy the waters of history, smudging the lens through which we view our past. Subsequently, like war, one of the first casualties of history is the truth, as it is routinely victimized by social architects and those who would sift it through a postmodern filter. Or worse, those historians, pundits, and politicians who purposefully revise the past in order to fit a present secular agenda or narrative. It's a sort of *verbal photoshopping* of history, with most unable to tell the difference between the real and the redacted. The result is a generation that neither knows history or understands our connection to it.

Case in point: During his presidency, while speaking at a

mosque in Baltimore, Barack Obama claimed that Islam has *always* been a part of America, and that it had been "woven into the fabric of our country since its founding." But a check into the facts reveals that this is, in fact, not true. Some slaves brought from Africa were indeed Muslim, and ironically, they were sold by Muslim slave traders. But apart from a percentage of slaves brought from Africa, where Islam was a prevailing influence, Muslims were practically nonexistent in America's beginnings.[4] Unless of course, you count the Barbary pirates the US encountered and with whom we fought two wars. These marauding sailors were from Morocco, Algeria, Tunis, and Tripoli—the Barbary Coast states. This early form of state-sponsored terrorism included attacking American merchant vessels on the open seas and holding Americans hostage for years. Because of her independence, the US was no longer protected by the British navy. Thus it took two wars (1801–1805, 1815–1816) to finally defeat these Muslim pirates.[5]

The first mosques did not appear in America until the first quarter of the twentieth century. So Obama's rewritten version of history totally missed the mark. But it served his narrative for the moment, helping to counter against a stereotype of Islam as a religion of terror, while simultaneously endearing himself to Muslims. The problem is that when presidents (and even pastors) revise history in order to legitimize or illustrate a point, many will take what they say as *gospel*.

Spiritual Amnesia

American philosopher George Santayana wrote, "Those who cannot remember the past are condemned to repeat it."[6]

Like a loop, history's events and experiences are replayed over and over again by those who fail to take into account the tragic mistakes of their predecessors. But Santayana's famous quote is more than a modern proverb of sorts. It also reflects a biblical principle.

Prior to their entrance into the Land of Promise following almost 40 years of meandering aimlessly in the Sinai desert, the Lord God spoke to Moses. The fruit of that monologue was the book of Deuteronomy, itself a historical recounting of previous revelation concerning the Law. And what was of utmost importance to Yahweh in this book? That His people not forget either the mistakes of their past nor the greatness of their God, in order that they may obey Him in the future.

> For what great nation is there that has a god so near to it as is the LORD our God whenever we call on Him? Or what great nation is there that has statutes and judgments as righteous as this whole law which I am setting before you today? Only give heed to yourself and keep your soul diligently, so that you *do not forget* the things which your eyes have seen and they *do not depart from your heart* all the days of your life; *but make them known* to your sons and your grandsons. *Remember...* (Deuteronomy 4:7-10).

Even their gracious and generous treatment of voluntary servants was based on *remembering* their own past experience in servitude:

> Remember that you were a slave in the land of Egypt, and the LORD your God brought you out of there by a mighty hand...therefore the LORD your God commanded you to observe the sabbath day (Deuteronomy 5:15).

However, just a half-century later, Israel's failure to recall the Lord's goodness, along with the people's own weakness toward sin, plunged them into a dark period of history. The era of the Judges is the chapter in Jewish history that chronicles their repeated sin and servitude. This collective spiritual amnesia went on for about 400 years. Their failure to learn from the past led them into oppression and enslavement by pagan nations and peoples.

Again and again, Israel was reminded to *remember*. For the Hebrew people, the perpetuation of truth, accurately transmitted from generation to generation, was essential to preserving not only their way of life, but also their very relationship with God.[7] That transmission is what we now call the Old Testament.

Fast-forward to the first century. Jesus, in His inauguration and establishment of the Lord's Supper, asked His disciples to observe it "in *remembrance* of Me."[8] In fact, Scripture has quite a bit to say about remembering the past as a way to enjoy God's love and provision in the present.[9]

I once saw a parody motivation poster that portrayed a picture of a sinking ship. Below the photo, in bold capital letters, was the word *MISTAKE* followed by, "It could be that the purpose of your life is only to serve as a warning to others."

Definitely *not* the legacy you're hoping for your life. And yet admittedly, we who follow Christ still suffer from spiritual blackouts and blind spots when it comes to remembering our past— including the tragic consequences of sin, God's goodness and grace, and our unwillingness to walk in His truth. And as it applies to America, it's simple, really. We're a nation of sinners.[10] A country populated with people romantically in love with their own hearts. Collectively, we're enslaved to a sin nature that both passively and actively resists, rejects, and runs from God.

Upon reflection, Santayana's words continue speaking to each new generation of Americans. To varying degrees, we practice the same sins as our ancestors, yet somehow expect different consequences. To the contrary, we end up condemning ourselves to the same fate. Sometimes even those who *do* learn from history end up repeating it anyway due to the expediency of the moment or a pride that rationalizes sin. "It won't happen to me. Not this time. Not to *my* generation."

Famous last words.

Clearly, when we miss the truth about our history, we become confused about its veracity and application to our lives today. So what is true about America's past? What can we really know about our biblical roots, if anything? And what is there about our country's past that is worthy of remembrance and imitation, particularly as it relates to our Christian heritage?

America a "Christian Nation"?

How did the United States begin? Upon what were we built? Are we really a "Christian nation," or has that claim been overstated for political and religious reasons in recent years? Have Christians been guilty of producing a skewed version of history? Have we erroneously, retroactively written our faith into the founding documents? Or are our religious roots being buried by revisionists under the soil of secularism? Let's transport our minds backward in time for a bit and recall what we know.

You may remember from American history class that pilgrim Separatists left England for Holland in 1608, escaping the impurities they saw in the Church of England. In their minds, they were convinced the official state church failed to reform still-pervasive Catholic traditions. Earlier, there had been a pivotal transition from Catholicism to Protestantism, beginning in 1534 with King Henry VIII's Act of Supremacy.[11] In this edict, King Henry VIII declared *himself* as the "only supreme head on earth of the Church of England."[12] But apart from officially breaking with Rome and the Pope, the church nonetheless remained largely Catholic in practice, propagating such beliefs and rituals as transubstantiation (the belief that during holy communion, the bread and wine are miraculously transformed into the body and blood of Jesus), private confession to priests, celibacy for clergy, and private masses.[13] Failure to believe in transubstantiation resulted in being burned at the stake. To unlawfully break the other requirements meant having your property seized, and upon the second offense, being executed as a felon.

But in Holland, the pilgrims were free to worship as they pleased. However, in relocating to that country, they soon found life there unsuitable as well—not only because opportunity for work was scarce, but also because they soon perceived Dutch culture to be a threat to their children's spiritual development. William Bradford, who later sailed on the Mayflower and eventually became Plymouth Plantation's governor, wrote concerning life in Holland,

> Of all the challenges to be borne [in Holland], was that many of the children, influenced by these conditions, and the great licentiousness of the young people of the country, and the many temptations of the city, were led by evil example into dangerous courses, getting the reins off their necks and leaving their parents. Some became soldiers, others embarked upon voyages by sea and others upon worse courses tending to dissoluteness and the danger of their souls, to the great grief of the parents and the dishonour of God. So they saw their posterity would be in danger to degenerate and become corrupt.[14]

Puritans (called such because they sought to purify the Church of England) left England and set sail for America in 1630, ten years after the pilgrims did. They also were of the conviction that there were too many unbiblical, Catholic traditions and influences in the Church of England. And because the church and government were so intertwined, to disobey the church meant disobedience to the king. This motivated them to seek a new home where they could practice their faith without hindrance, worldly influence, or fear of persecution.

So America's pioneer settlers were predominantly Christian, searching for a land in which they could practice their faith without interference or influence from government control. Early religious life in the new world was overwhelmingly Protestant, with a strong Puritan heritage, largely defined by Anglican, Presbyterian, Congregationalist, Baptist, and Quaker churches. However, over time, allegiance to God and the church's influence on colonialists' lives began to weaken. Their original dream to establish a godly nation and a "city set on a hill" had become second to making a living and enjoying life in the colonies. Like many churches today, congregations became lifeless and lukewarm.

Then came the Great Awakening.

Beginning with Dutch Reformed minister Theodore Frelinghuysen, and gaining momentum through Jonathan Edwards, George Whitfield, and the Wesley brothers, widespread revival broke out across the colonies. Thousands were converted and churches were invigorated, experiencing new life. The effect on public life was noticeable. An emphasis on missions was born, bringing the gospel to Native Americans and African slaves. Young men began to aspire to the ministry, and this created a need to educate them. Institutions like Princeton, Rutgers, Brown, and Dartmouth universities were all established as a direct result of the Great Awakening.[15]

Thousands came to hear George Whitfield preach. Because of his notoriety among the people, he captured the attention of a Philadelphia printer named Benjamin Franklin. Franklin admired the preacher's speaking ability and his impact on those who heard him speak. Though many theologians and historians question whether Franklin ever actually came to saving faith in Jesus Christ, he and Whitfield nevertheless became lifelong friends.[16] Franklin even contributed to Whitfield's ministry on occasion and also published Whitfield's sermons. In his autobiography, Franklin recounted the impact America's spiritual awakening had on the nation, observing,

> It seem'd as if all the world were growing Religious; so that one could not walk thro' the Town in an evening without hearing Psalms sung in different families of every Street.[17]

But though God's Spirit was moving throughout the colonies for the gospel, trouble was brewing on a national level. Governments were mostly local, with most communities led by governors elected by legislature or landowners. For a time, England had practiced somewhat of a "hands off" policy, as it was preoccupied with affairs elsewhere. But in time, English regulations, including restrictions on trade and taxation, pushed the colonialists to the breaking point. The result was the American Revolution.

Drafting what became known as the Constitution, the founding fathers conceived the following preamble,

> We the People of the United States, in Order to form a more perfect Union, establish Justice, insure domestic Tranquility, provide for the common defence, promote the general Welfare, and secure the Blessings of Liberty to ourselves and our Posterity, do ordain and establish this Constitution for the United States of America.[18]

Thus began the great document upon which our country was founded. However, today's debate over the founding fathers' intentions when forming that "more perfect Union" has ignited a firestorm of controversy. On one side are those who deny any substantive religious intent whatsoever in the crafting of our founding documents. On the other end of the spectrum are those who insist the United States of America was unmistakably begun as a Christian nation.

So who's right? And just what do we mean by the phrase *Christian nation* anyway? Is it possible that *both* perspectives somehow touch on the truth? Or is one more prominent than the other?

It would obviously require more than a single chapter (or book) to explore the annals of history, uncovering every shred of evidence related to the role of Christianity in America's beginning. And even then, we would still be forced to sift through the digested opinions of historians, educators, activists, constitutional lawyers, judges, and theologians. This chapter will not end that debate or become the definitive word on the subject.

But it will address a fundamental question: What do we mean when we say America was founded as a Christian nation? What does that phrase imply? There are several interpretive options here. Christian nation *could* mean:

1. Every American citizen is a Christian.

2. Every citizen is required to believe Christian theology.

3. America's founding fathers were all committed Christians.

4. The founders intended for Christianity to be the state religion.

5. The majority religion of the country was Christianity at the time.

6. Our heritage wasn't Jewish, Muslim, or Hindu, so the only religion left is Christianity.

7. The Bible and a Christian worldview helped shape our country's beginning.

Of all the possibilities, number 7 seems to be the most reasonable, and here's why: When attempting to understand and interpret historical events or documents (including the Bible), *context* is everything. We must avoid viewing history through a contemporary lens and judging our ancestors too harshly. The times in which they lived—world events, crises, predominant views regarding science and God, perceived threats to national security, economic conditions, social customs, and way of life—all factor into fairly and accurately understanding both the *what* and *why* of the past.

Therefore, it's important to frame our minds as best we can with the worldview of *their* day, not ours. Again, all contributing influences cannot be explored here. But take, for example, that in the late 1700s, the cultural context in which America's great founding documents were penned, notwithstanding the Enlightenment, was a time when our nation's founders recognized and affirmed *biblical* values. This is not to say they all were great spiritual leaders. It *is* to say, however, that it's unthinkable to imagine them allowing, condoning, and celebrating such things as homosexual marriage or the right of mothers to slaughter their unborn children by the thousands each day in our country. Were such vile practices carried out back then, the founding fathers would have flipped their powdered wigs!

And exactly *why* would these men have been opposed to such things? Was it because they were simply lagging behind the rest of the world when it comes to tolerance, equality, and women's rights? No. It was because Western civilization, as a whole, was *Christianized*. And America's spiritual emerging, though still clearly in its infancy, nevertheless was marked by a common worldview that promoted and harmonized with Christian dignity, decency, and morality. This doesn't mean all Americans were Christians, but rather, that the guiding light of liberty was lit in the undeniable context of a God-consciousness, and that common-sense decency was rooted in biblical truth. Put simply, the canvas of Christianity was the backdrop on which the character of America was brushstroked.

Predictably, revisionist historians are quick to point out that there is no mention of God in the US Constitution, save for the final words: "done in Convention…the Seventeenth Day of September *in the Year of our Lord* one thousand seven hundred and Eighty seven and of the Independence of the United States of America."

However, what they often fail to mention is that prior to this, 11 years earlier, the Declaration of Independence, considered to be America's "articles of incorporation," mentions God 5 times, in the following contexts:

1. God as the *Source* of Common Grace—"Laws of Nature." Divinely appointed laws applicable and beneficial to all mankind.

2. God as *Creator/Sustainer* of the World—"Nature's God." The theory of evolution had yet to be conceived, as the founders clearly acknowledged the God of the Bible as the originator of life.

3. God as the *Giver* of Certain Rights—"We hold these truths to be self-evident, that all men are created equal, that they are endowed by their Creator with certain unalienable Rights, that among these are Life, Liberty and the pursuit of Happiness. — That to secure these rights, Governments are instituted among Men…"

Regarding this, Constitutional expert Dr. Harold Pease contends,

> So passionate were they [the framers of America's founding documents] with respect to these three "God-given rights" that such was identified as the *purpose of government*. "That to secure these rights, Governments are instituted among Men,

deriving their just powers from the consent of the governed…"[19]

In other words, government exercises a *God-given* stewardship, protecting the *God-given* rights of its citizens. That's government's purpose for existing.

4. God as *Judge*—The signers then appealed to the "Supreme Judge of the world" for assistance in fulfilling the intentions of breaking free from English rule.

5. God as *Sovereign Protector*—Finally, the Declaration's signers expressed their trust in Nature's God for protection as they pursue this course of action, "with a firm reliance on the protection of Divine Providence."

So this leads us to an important question: Precisely to which "God" were our country's founders referring? Was it Allah? Perhaps Confucius? Or maybe Buddha? Possibly Osiris? Or Zeus? Or the Flying Spaghetti Monster? No. It was blaringly obvious to any common man then—peasant or privileged—as well as any intelligent person today that the God and Creator to whom the fathers appealed was the God of the Christian Bible. And *no one* has yet to present a reasonable argument to the contrary, though some feebly try.

Bear in mind, of the 56 signers of the Declaration of Independence, only 2 were "professional ministers."[20] The rest were lawyers, landowners, merchants, doctors, scientists, and farmers. That theologians weren't needed to frame this document's reference and allegiance to God is significant and is testament to their belief in His existence and necessary involvement in the affairs of men and nations.

Obviously not all these men were Christian in all their beliefs and practices. In fact, many were decidedly influenced by the

Enlightenment and their vision to separate from what they believed was a *theocratic* dictatorship of England. There were certainly non-Christians of many varieties among the more than 140 signers of the Declaration of Independence, Articles of Confederation, and the Constitution, though virtually every one of them were affiliated with some denomination or sect of the Christian church.[21] Then, as now, men are motivated by self-serving interests, egos, and financial gain. And yet even a nonbeliever in Jefferson's day understood that the biblical principles of Christianity were what would secure and stabilize this new republic, and protect the rights and freedom of its citizens.

Jefferson himself explained to a friend while walking to church one Sunday,

> No nation has ever existed or been governed without religion. Nor can be. The Christian religion is the best religion that has been given to man and I, as Chief Magistrate of this nation, am bound to give it the sanction of my example.[22]

In defense of their honor and courage, upon putting pen to ink and signing the Declaration, these men acknowledged the risk inherent with such an act. By publicly absolving themselves of all allegiance to the British Crown, they were intentionally committing treason against England and its king, a crime punishable by death. And because they signed their own death warrant for the cause of freedom, they deserve our utmost respect and admiration.

In recent history, widely circulated folklore, radio broadcasts, military speeches, chain e-mails, and even sermons have perpetuated a story claiming that during the ensuing Revolutionary War, "nine of the Declaration's signers died of wounds or hardships, 17 lost everything that they owned, and five were imprisoned or captured," among many other personal losses and suffering. This story has proven to be largely apocryphal, as the vast majority of them managed to avoid capture, torture, and death at the hands of the British.[23] This in no way casts doubt on their courage or lessens their impact in that initial struggle for freedom and independence. Regardless of the uncertain outcome of their courageous treason, these men nevertheless stood strong, indelibly inking their names into the annals of history. Thank God they did!

Sifting Through the Fog

So in what sense can we confidently and truthfully say America was begun as a Christian nation? It certainly wasn't created as a theocratic state, meant to be governed by priests and ecclesiastical church leaders. And it is hardly supportable that the founders merely paid cultural lip service to God as America's foundations were being poured.

Consider the perspectives of key government leaders at the time of America's birth and infancy:

John Adams, our second president, said, "The general principles on which the fathers achieved independence were…the general principles of Christianity."[24]

In 1854, the House Judiciary Committee declared, in response to a push by some to remove religious influence in government,

> Had the people, during the Revolution, had a suspicion of any attempt to war against Christianity, that Revolution would have been strangled in its cradle. At the time of the adoption of the Constitution and the amendments, the universal sentiment was that Christianity should be encouraged, not any one sect [denomination]. Any attempt to level and discard all religion would have been viewed with universal indignation…In

this age there can be no substitute for Christianity; that, in its general principles, is the great conservative element on which we must rely for the purity and permanence of free institutions.[25]

Two years later, the House of Representatives stated, "The great vital and conservative element in our system is the belief of our people in the pure doctrines and divine truths of the Gospel of Jesus Christ."[26]

During the Civil War, President Abraham Lincoln called the entire nation not to a "moment of silence," but to a day of "national prayer and humiliation," writing,

> Sincerely believing that no people, however great in numbers and resources or however strong in the justice of their cause, can prosper without His favor; and at the same time deploring the national offences which have provoked His righteous judgment, yet encouraged in this day of trouble by the assurances of His word to seek Him for succor according to His appointed way through Jesus Christ, the Senate of the United States do hereby request the President of the United States, by his proclamation, to designate and set apart a day for national prayer and humiliation.[27]

Appointed by President James Madison, US Supreme Court justice Joseph Story noted,

> One of the beautiful boasts of our municipal jurisprudence is that Christianity is a part of the Common Law…There never has been a period in which the Common Law did not recognize Christianity as lying at its foundations…I verily believe Christianity necessary to the support of civil society.[28]

Supreme Court Justice John McLean, appointed in 1829 by President Andrew Jackson (who stated, "The Bible is the rock upon which our republic rests"), wrote,

> For many years, my hope for the perpetuity of our institutions has rested upon Bible morality and the general dissemination of Christian principles. This is an element which did not exist in the ancient republics. It is a basis on which free governments may be maintained through all time…Free government is not a self-moving machine…Our mission of freedom is not carried out by brute force, by canon law, or *any other law except the moral law and those Christian principles which are found in the Scriptures.*[29]

George Washington said, "It is the duty of all nations to acknowledge the providence of Almighty God, to obey His will, to be grateful for His benefits, and humbly to implore His protection and favor."[30] In his personal prayer journal, Washington wrote,

> Oh, eternal and everlasting God, direct my thoughts, words and work. Wash away my sins in the immaculate blood of the Lamb and purge my heart by Thy Holy Spirit. Daily, frame me more and more in the likeness of Thy son, Jesus Christ, that living in Thy fear, and dying in Thy favor, I may in Thy appointed time obtain the resurrection of the justified unto eternal life. Bless, O Lord, the whole race of mankind and let the world be filled with the knowledge of Thee and Thy son, Jesus Christ.

John Jay, the first US Supreme Court justice, said, "Providence has given to our people the choice of their rulers, and it is their duty—as well as privilege and interest—of our Christian nation to select and prefer Christians for their rulers."[31]

Founding father Benjamin Rush said, "The only foundation for…a republic is to be laid in Religion. Without this there can be no virtue, and without virtue there can be no liberty, and liberty is the object and life of all republican governments."[32]

Finally, in his book, *The United States: A Christian Nation*, Justice David Brewer wrote,

> We classify nations in various ways: as, for instance, by their form of government. One is a kingdom, another an empire, and still another a republic. Also by race. Great Britain is an Anglo-Saxon nation, France a Gallio, Germany a Teutonic, Russia a Slav. And still again by religion. One is a Mohammedan nation, others are heathen, and still others are Christian nations.
>
> This republic is classified among the Christian nations of the world. It was so formally declared by the Supreme Court of the United States. In the case of Holy Trinity Church vs. United States, 143 U.S. 471, that Court, after mentioning various circumstances, added, "these and many other matters which might be noticed, add a volume of unofficial declarations to the mass of organic utterances that this is a Christian nation."

He continued,

> I have said enough to show that Christianity came to this country with the first colonists; has been powerfully identified with its rapid development, colonial and national, and today exists as a mighty factor in the life of the republic. This is a Christian nation…the calling of this republic a Christian nation is not a mere pretence, but a recognition of an historical, legal, and social truth.[33]

Space does not permit me to catalogue an exhaustive list of quotes from presidents, justices, statesmen, and other government leaders instrumental in the founding and formation of our country.[34]

Let it be noted that these are not the blog posts of twenty-first-century right-wing, agenda-driven, conservative pundits, but rather the unquestionable beliefs of men who were intricately involved in the founding and formation of our country. They are neither recent concepts, nor are they reinterpreted for contemporary convenience.

And where else might we find evidence of our uniquely Christian foundation? Perhaps nowhere is this reality more documented than in, of all places, Washington, DC itself. Hung in galleries, carved out of stone, and sandblasted into buildings are permanent, perpetual reminders of who we once aspired to be as a nation. More than preserved ancient documents that fade or are forgotten over time, chiseled into marble in America's capital are found rock-solid testimonies to our country's spiritual foundations.

In Washington, DC you can find the following:

The Capitol Building—Eight huge paintings depicting various aspects of our Christian heritage, including the baptism of the first convert along with the reading of Scripture.

The Library of Congress—On display in climate-controlled cases are a Gutenberg Bible and a Giant Bible of Mainz. Scripture is inscribed on the ceilings and walls, and statues of Moses and Paul can be found in the Main Reading Room.

The National Archives—The Ten Commandments are embossed in bronze in the floor of the main rotunda.

The Lincoln Memorial—The sixteenth president's own words are engraved upon the marble walls of this great monument, and include references to Scripture, prayer, and God's providence—evidence of Lincoln's strong faith and its application to us as a nation.

The Jefferson Memorial—Inscriptions can be seen that reflect America's strong ties to God, including Jefferson's words, "God who gave us life gave us liberty. Can the liberties of a nation be secure when we have removed a conviction that these liberties are the gift of God? Indeed, I tremble for my country when I reflect that God is just, that his justice cannot sleep forever."

The Washington Monument—Atop the east side of this grand 555-foot marble/granite structure can be found an inscription on the aluminum capstone that reads, "Laus Deo," which is Latin for "Praise Be to God."

The Supreme Court—America's justice system owes its existence to a Judeo-Christian foundation. The oak doors leading into the court chamber are engraved with the Roman numerals I through X, alluding to the Ten Commandments. On the east pediment of the building is a prominent marble relief of Moses holding the Ten Commandments.

The White House—John Adams, the first president to occupy the White House, wrote to his wife on November 2, 1800, "I pray Heaven to bestow the best of Blessings on this House and on all that shall hereafter inhabit it. May none but honest and wise Men ever rule under this roof."

During World War II, and not long before his death, President Franklin Roosevelt had John Adam's words carved into the stone fireplace in the State Dining Room.

So it is indisputable that, since her founding, the United States of America has unashamedly acknowledged the Judeo-Christian God of heaven. Therefore it is foolish to acknowledge or believe the rantings of secular historians or follow the folly of political rhetoric that seeks to rewrite the account of America's beginnings or to redefine her original identity. Simply trace the spirit of America, and you will find a strong awareness of God as she began her historical three-century journey. Aside from being founded as an ecclesiastical state, America has enjoyed about as much of a biblical beginning as a country could have.

Historian Will Durant, himself an atheist, wrote, "Even the skeptical historian develops a humble respect for religion, since he sees it functioning, and seemingly indispensable, in every land and age…There is no significant example in history, before our time, of a society successfully maintaining moral life without the aid of religion."[35]

Our founding fathers wisely understood this. While not painting them as twenty-first-century right-wing, conservative evangelicals, the fact remains that our nation's founders were, by and large, God-fearing men with a deep respect for Scripture and a commitment to religious freedom. They did not intend to create a state religion, enforcing its values as law, and punishing those who refuse to believe its tenets. However, they did purposefully align our nation's foundation with the cornerstone of a biblical framework, basic Christian morality, and civil behavior. They recognized that Christianity alone provides the best principles upon which to found and govern a nation.

But when America looks in the mirror today, does she even recognize herself anymore? And does it even matter whether or not we were founded as a Christian-based nation? What difference does it make whether we can prove we once had biblical beginnings? On the one hand it matters greatly, as this enables us to call our country back to its true, original identity. But on the other hand, regardless of how we began, we still have a critical need to repent and turn the nation toward God. No matter what the actual *degree* of Christian influence the founding fathers *intended*, it changes nothing of the need for today's America to anchor herself to godly principles of decency, morality, and justice.

In an effort to combat the insanity and immorality of a post-modern, post-Christian America, conservative Christians often cling to the adage, "But we were founded as a *Christian nation...*" And, as we've seen, that claim has great merit. But even if it didn't, we would still need to call our country to repentance.

What those early pioneers and founding fathers could not have possibly known is how the infant nation they helped birth would grow and change in the subsequent two-and-a-half centuries. How would they respond if they knew America was losing all chances of ever returning to what once made her great?

3

LESSONS FROM AN
ANCIENT PEOPLE

I will bless those who bless you,
and the one who curses you I will curse.

—GENESIS 12:3

On April 8, 1630, a fleet of four English ships set sail from Yarmouth, Isle of Wight. Bound for the new world, these four would be followed a month later by seven more vessels. All told, around seven hundred passengers—men, women, and children—were on board the eleven ships. During their long journey, they encountered bitter cold, rain, storms lasting for days, gale-force winds, and sickness. Some were born during the voyages, while others died. However, nine weeks later, and much to the relief of all, they finally made land in Salem, Massachusetts.

Among the passengers of this historic crossing was John Winthrop, an English Puritan. A lawyer by profession, Winthrop also served as the leader of this adventurous band of immigrants, and would later be elected as governor of the Massachusetts Bay Colony. Winthrop was aboard the flagship *Arbella*, and at some point in their long voyage, saw fit to deliver a timely sermon to his fellow pilgrim travelers in an effort to help prepare them for life in the new land. In his message, entitled "The Model of Christian Charity," Winthrop outlined his vision for survival and success upon their arrival, which included the necessity of sharing goods and bearing one another's burdens in what would be a challenging and harsh new environment. Winthrop actually saw this new endeavor as a "covenant" between the English settlers and God, which, if successful, he believed would guarantee the Lord's blessings. He also urged them to "follow the counsel of Micah, to do justly, to love mercy and walk humbly with our God."[1] However, failure to obey would cause Him to withdraw His favor and instead, bring His judgment.

At the close of his now-famous sermon, Winthrop concluded,

> We shall find that the God of Israel is among us, when ten of us shall be able to resist a thousand of our enemies; when He shall make us a praise and glory that men shall say of succeeding plantations, "may the Lord make it like that of New England." For we must consider that we shall be as a *city upon a hill*. The eyes of all people are upon us. So that if we shall deal falsely with our God in this work we have undertaken, and so cause Him to withdraw His present help from us, we shall be made a story and a by-word through the world.[2]

Their passage from England, later known as part of the Great Migration, had, at its core, not only a desire to start a new life in an uncharted land, but to do their part in advancing and perhaps even ushering in the kingdom of God itself. With Winthrop's vision of this new Christian colony as a "city upon a hill," an intentional biblical parallel was drawn and applied, comparing them to ancient Israel's possession of the Land. He also painted a portrait of a people who could perhaps fulfill Christ's vision of reigning on earth through establishing a Christian society. However, this idea of bringing in the kingdom of God on earth did not begin with Winthrop. Reformers and theologians like John Calvin and John Owen also subscribed to this belief.[3]

A friend of Winthrop and the Massachusetts Bay Colony was clergyman John Cotton. Coinciding with Winthrop's departure from Yarmouth, Cotton travelled to Southampton to preach a farewell sermon to his native England. Entitled "God's Promise to His Plantation," the minister not only argued for the "divine right" to occupy the new land, but also portrayed strong similarities between the Puritans and God's chosen people in the Old Testament. "Taking the land" like Israel did the Promised Land was more than just a passing metaphor to Cotton. It was part of his theology. Mirroring Israel's possession of Canaan, the Puritans' vision of life in the new continent would bring to fruition the Reformers' work in the church.

Both Winthrop and Cotton helped lead this charge across an ideological ocean to a new way of thinking about the church's role in society. Christianizing the New World, for them, meant bringing about a society where righteousness reigned and God was honored by the masses, thus ushering in a "Golden Age of Christianity." It was an optimistic prospect, and we would surely join them in their desire to see those "in the wilderness" embrace salvation through Jesus.

But as noble as their motivation may have been, their failure to make clear distinctions between Israel, government, and the church was both an interpretative and theological mistake. It was also a practical improbability. Not to judge them too harshly, though. To be fair, every generation of Christians, from centuries one to twenty-one, has been influenced by the times in which they have lived.

Governments, national cultures, and the state of the world in every era have all played a part in how we Christians have viewed God's kingdom plan, the end times, and our role in them. This has perhaps never been so true as it is today. But it is precisely why contemporary prophecy experts (yours truly included) must take great care in avoiding sensationalism and extrabiblical speculation. Those of us who believe we actually are living in the last days must exercise caution so as not to unnecessarily read too much of our own times into Scripture. The Bible must always be the filter through which we interpret culture, not vice-versa.

That being said, Winthrop's and Cotton's sermons are but representations of a mindset prevalent among those early Puritan pilgrims. But Scripture does not teach that the church is either an extension or a rebirth of the nation Israel.[4] Jesus commanded us to take the gospel into all the world, but we do not have a divine mandate to also take the *land* through some sort of theocratic domination. Unfortunately, this belief is still propagated by some fringe Christian groups today.[5] Sadly, many pastors have even launched building campaigns, employing metaphorical "Take the Land" or "Get to the Promised Land" slogans and sermons to inspire their congregations and motivate financial pledges. In more recent history, the "city upon a hill" description has been used by presidents from Kennedy to Reagan, though applied more toward America's exceptionalism than to our country being some sort of New Jerusalem.

An Elevated Perspective

When viewed on the timeline of recorded history, the United States is, at under 250 years old, a relatively young country, especially when compared to nations like Japan, Greece, China, or Egypt. But it's not America's short history that makes us unique. Rather it's what our country has become in that short time. Our nation has been *the* world leader in promoting freedom and providing its citizens the opportunity to pursue life and happiness. We are a republic that possesses great resources, an abundance of which we have shared with the world. America's military has proven to be unmatched. Rather than going forth to expand our empire and conquer nations, we instead liberate them from their oppressors. America has led the way in saving the planet from tyranny in two World Wars *and* the Cold War. We are among the most prosperous, yet generous nations on earth. We have pioneered unrivalled advances in medicine and technology.

We've even gone to the moon—six times.

Of all nations, the United States has had an immeasurable impact on the course of recent history. And the world would be a drastically different place had she not been born. But along with our rapid growth, development, and global prominence is an underlying notion that makes us think we are somehow the center of the universe. In terms of world events, we tend to be less globally conscious and more *ethno*centric. This may stem from a perpetuated independent spirit lingering from our Revolutionary beginnings. More likely it is because of the fact that we have been, historically, a self-sufficient people. After all, we're *Americans*, right? We don't typically ask for help. We have wealth and abundant resources. We're rich in food, industry, and technology. Unlike stores in other countries, our grocery shelves are perpetually stocked. Our roads are paved. Our hospitals, unrivalled globally. Our technology, state of the art. Our entertainment, the best. We have everything we need here.

Unfortunately, America's general populace today knows more about technology than they do their own history, and even less about world history. We are much more educated in the here and now than the *there and then*. And yet, though we may lag behind in education, we nevertheless still excel in other areas. Opportunity and freedom have remained our calling cards for well over 200 years.

But with all her greatness, the bubble of America's preeminence bursts when we realize we are *not* the focal point of history. Though our wonderful country has been fortunate and blessed, we are not "God's chosen people." We are a country—exceptional and unique, but still just a country. This neither demeans who we are nor diminishes our accomplishments and rich heritage. On the contrary, it puts them into a healthy perspective. For we cannot properly understand America's past, present, *or* future without also understanding the nature of who she is and what role she plays in history.

I was reminded of this not long ago while watching a video produced by the American Museum of Natural History. I have always been fascinated with outer space, and where I live, there are no city lights to hide the night sky. I often find myself gazing into the heavenly expanse, pondering the greatness of God. But this video was a digital animation portraying the grandeur of outer space. It began with a bird's-eye view from above the Himalaya mountains. Then the lens began moving backward, panning the horizon, past earth's atmosphere and the planet itself. The lens continued moving back, past the moon. Soon it journeyed across the known planets. It kept travelling away from earth, beyond our solar system, constellations, and billions of stars onward. Proceeding further into space, it took me light-years away in time and travel. Then it left our galaxy, the Milky Way, after which it passed by other mapped galaxies. Then on into the emptiness of the universe where I encountered quasars, distant objects so bright they "eclipse the ancient galaxies that contain them, and are powered by black holes a billion times as massive as our sun."[6]

I found this video overwhelming, and admittedly a bit disturbing. It caused me to feel the lonely, cold emptiness of space. The farther I travelled, and the more I saw of the utter vastness of space, the smaller and more insignificant I felt. It made me realize that the earth, though massive when compared to myself, is but a miniscule dust-speck in the universe. And at least from a physical/spatial standpoint, it's really not that important compared to the grand scope of creation. Thankfully, the God who made it all deeply cares for us and loves us!

But the knowledge and feeling that accompanied watching this video gave me a sense of *perspective*. And that's something we desperately need when thinking about countries like ours. Fortunately, God is in the business of giving us His perspective through His Word. Using Scripture, our minds are elevated far above our present time and the confusing cloud-fog that often accompanies it. Getting into the Word helps us to see ourselves, our country, and our world from His vantage point. It's a panoramic view that prevents us from unnecessarily downplaying our role or inflating it. More importantly, it helps us accurately understand God's relationship to the nations, including America. And that's what we desperately need at the moment—heaven's perspective on the United States.

Promise Is a Promise

Before Israel was born through Abraham, God dealt with humanity through divine revelation given to Adam, which was faithfully passed down to his descendants. Because God is Creator of all mankind, He requires all men to obey that revelation and the moral law written in the conscience. When humanity did not comply, He brought devastating judgment. You remember the Flood story, don't you? So since creation, God has dealt with humanity on the basis of both natural and divine revelation. What can be known about Him in nature and what He has revealed to men are His primary ways of telling us who He is and what He requires of us.

Oftentimes God has communicated directly with individuals, choosing them for specific tasks. One of these men was Noah, through whom He warned the world of that impending global flood.[7] Noah built an ark of salvation to deliver a remnant from God's coming wrath. About 300 years after this horrific judgment that destroyed a depraved human race, God's revelation came once again to another lone individual. Like Noah, this man was also chosen to provide a way of salvation for humanity. However, *unlike* Noah, this man would produce a *people*, not a boat. His name was Abram, later changed by God to Abraham.[8] And while the ark builder had benefitted from a long heritage of godly men going back for well over a millennium, Abram's family was decidedly pagan in origin. Having come from Ur of the Chaldees, Abraham's family were likely worshippers of Nanna, the moon god, and who was their chief deity.[9] Nevertheless, Yahweh's sovereign call came to this man, initiating what would become the birth of the Jewish nation and a prophetic fountainhead of our salvation. Moses records for us this historic episode:

> The LORD had said to Abram, "Go from your country, your people and your father's household to the land I will show you.
>
> "I will make you into a great nation,
> and I will bless you;
> I will make your name great,
> and you will be a blessing.
> I will bless those who bless you,
> and whoever curses you I will curse;
> and all peoples on earth
> will be blessed through you" (Genesis 12:1-3 NIV).[10]

Through carefully examining the Lord's prophecy to Abraham,

we discover several important aspects of this promise known as the Abrahamic Covenant.

First, it was a *specific* promise.

The covenant that God inaugurated here was to Abraham alone. Out of all the people on earth, heaven again chose one individual. Like Noah, Abraham would be an instrument of God to the nations. However, again, contrasting Noah's experience, prior to this revelation Abraham had no experiential knowledge of Yahweh. And therefore God's promise to this individual was, by necessity, direct and definitive. In it, the Lord itemized exactly what He wanted Abraham to do as well as what *He* intended to do for him. Whereas God's pledge to Abraham initially came in Genesis 12, the covenant was further confirmed and ratified in Genesis 15 and 17. Stephen tells us God originally appeared to Abraham prior to Genesis 12, while he was still in the land of the Chaldeans (Mesopotamia).[11] But like other promises and prophecies in Scripture, this revelation to Abraham was given progressively and repeatedly over time. It also included a geographical inheritance involving a land with specific boundaries.[12] Therefore, this prophetic word became God's promissory note for the Promised Land.

Second, it was an *unconditional* promise.

In Abraham's day as in ours, covenants (contracts) required signatures from *two* parties in order for them to become legal and binding. However, curiously, the promise God made with Abraham and his descendants would break with this tradition. Abraham had asked the Lord, "How may I know that I will possess [the land]?"[13] God replied by telling him to go get a heifer, a goat, a ram, a turtledove, and a young pigeon. God then took the animals and cut them into two halves.[14] He then put Abraham into a deep sleep, speaking to him in a vision.[15] After this, a smoking oven and a flaming torch appeared. These were symbols of Yahweh's righteous presence.[16] At that point, the oven and torch passed through the middle of the animal parts. The custom of the day was that when two men agreed on a covenant contract, they would split an animal in two and then walk together between the parts, pledging that if either of them broke the agreement, the same bloody fate would befall them.[17] But here, *only God* bound Himself to the promise by passing between the halves alone. Genesis 15:18 states, "On that day the LORD made a covenant with Abram."

The verb translated "made a covenant" literally means to "*cut* a covenant" in Hebrew, referring to the bloody custom of securing agreements in that day. But Abraham was passive in the making of this covenant, as God alone passed between the animal parts. God's promise would therefore be without conditions, and its ultimate fulfillment would depend solely upon Him. Abraham's part was to simply *believe* (verse 6). And even though in future generations Israel would prove to be disobedient, their unfaithfulness did not nullify the unconditional nature of this particular covenant.[18]

Third, it was an *everlasting* promise.

Years later, the Lord reappeared to Abraham, further confirming the prophecy promise He previously made to him. This is when the Lord officially changed Abram's name to Abraham.[19] And it is here God declared,

> I will establish my covenant as an *everlasting* covenant between me and you and your descendants after you for the generations to come, to be your God and the God of your descendants after you. The whole land of Canaan, where you now reside as a foreigner, I will give as an *everlasting* possession to you and your descendants after you; and I will be their God (Genesis 17:7-8).

Attempts to spiritualize the word "everlasting" or to explain it away come up short, as this word is deep within the clear context of other literal promises God made to Abraham. The promise to "establish my covenant between Me and you" (17:2) was literal. His promise to "multiply you exceedingly" (verse 2) was literal. His covenant to make him a "father of a multitude of nations" (verse 5) was literal. God did not intend to give Abraham imaginary descendants, but actual ones. The land He promised was a *physical* land, and its boundaries, precise. Every one of these guarantees from God to Abraham was literal in both their intent and in their fulfillment. Therefore, the promise to possess that land would also be an *everlasting* promise. God later repeated this, again referring to it as an "everlasting covenant," and the land a gift for an "everlasting possession."[20]

So why is all this so important? Why dwell on an ancient Jewish covenant when talking about twenty-first-century America? As believers living in the last days, we must understand that for 20 centuries, Abraham's seed (Israel) has *not* possessed the land God promised to them. But in recent history, something supernatural and prophetic occurred. In the mid-twentieth century, Jews began flooding back to the Promised Land due to Israel becoming a nation again on May 14, 1948. This is a prophecy being fulfilled before our very eyes, and one that will be finally realized when Christ returns and inaugurates His literal reign on earth during the millennial kingdom.[21]

You may remember that when Joshua led Israel to conquer and possess the land, the people's disobedience eventually led them into dispersion and captivity. Though many Jews were allowed to return to Jerusalem and the land following their captivity by Babylon and Persia, not all did. And those who did certainly did not go on to possess it *indefinitely* (everlasting). Then, in AD 70, Jerusalem and the Jewish temple were destroyed by the Roman general Titus.[22] Thus began for the Jews a worldwide dispersion lasting 2000 years. In fact, for the first time since Bible times, there are more Jews living in the land promised to Abraham than anywhere else in the world.[23] This, I believe, not only is setting the stage for the time of Antichrist and Tribulation, but it also illustrates the Jewish people's undeniable compulsion to return home. It's also a partial, ongoing fulfillment of Bible prophecy.

Fourth, it was a *rewarding* promise.

When God declared to Abraham that He would "bless those who bless you, and the one who curses you I will curse," He really meant it. And literally. God's divine protection for Abraham and his descendants was an integral part of His covenant with him (Genesis 15:1). Part of that protection involved rewarding nations if they treated Abraham and his descendants fairly, or alternatively bringing judgment if they mistreated the patriarch and the nation that would eventually come from his seed. In fact, within the covenant itself, God prophesied judgment on Egypt for that country's future enslavement of the Jewish people (verses 13-14). And so it has been for all those who have treated the Jews harshly, not only in biblical times but in modern times as well.[24]

The list of Israel's enemies and oppressors reads like an Obituary of Empires: Egypt. Assyria. Babylon. Medo-Persia. The Amalekites. The Ammonites. The Philistines (run into any Philistines lately?). The Edomites. The Moabites. Rome. Some of these kingdoms and peoples lost their dominance as a world power. Some were conquered by other nations. And still others were wiped from the pages of history altogether. You can attempt to explain their collective demise any way you wish. But I call it a divine coincidence that what they all share in common is a mistreatment or oppression of the Jewish people. The same will one day be said of those countries which come against Israel in the last days.

In the late nineteenth century, a movement was begun of Jewish people returning and reestablishing a home in their ancient land. Going into the twentieth century, the Zionist movement gained momentum. But then WW2 happened, and nearly 6 million Jews were annihilated. This casualty of evil showcased the Jewish people's need for a home of their own. Led by Dr. Chaim Weizmann, president of the World Zionist Organization, a proposal for the new state of Israel was drafted but originally rejected by President Truman.

However, in a quirk of history, an obscure man named Eddie Jacobson, one of Truman's best friends since childhood, secured a private meeting with the president. Himself a Jew, Jacobson appealed to Truman, finally persuading him to support the proposal. It all culminated with a Declaration of Independence on May 14, 1948. On that day the nation of Israel was born *again* and officially established in the modern world. Just eleven minutes after the declaration, President Harry S. Truman issued a statement recognizing "the provisional government as the de facto authority of the new State of Israel."[25] And for the most part, the United States has been a strong supporter and friend of Israel since that day.

Though our government has not always been in sync with every political and military decision Israel has made the last 70 years, the United States of America has remained that tiny nation's strongest world ally. This is particularly significant in light of the presently growing European anti-Semitism and a host of nations surrounding Israel who are poised and ready to do battle with the Jewish state. While chanting "death to Israel," and calling for Jewish extermination, these Muslim countries wish to wipe Israel off the map, vowing to finish the job Hitler started.[26]

Here at home, the Unites States has "blessed" Israel rather than cursing her as other countries have done. That, many Bible teachers say, may account for some of the heavenly favor America has enjoyed.

Fifth, it was a *redemptive* promise.

A final aspect of the covenant God made with Abraham was that it prophesied, in time, that the Messiah would come from His lineage: "In you all the families [nations] of the earth will be blessed" (Genesis 12:3).

The truth of this prophetic promise is abundantly repeated throughout Scripture.[27] And the original covenant contained a promise of salvation whose fulfillment would eventually reach to the whole world, including people from "every nation and all tribes and peoples and tongues."[28]

It was a mighty covenant made by an almighty God. A promise that was specific, unconditional, everlasting, rewarding, and redemptive. If it is possible for us to spiritualize God's covenant to Abraham, then we could also spiritualize other promises, including those God has made to the church. There are theologians today who assert that there are no valid promises still in effect for Israel today. Through attaching relative or conditional meaning to God's covenant with Abraham, many believe the *church* to be "the new Israel."

But the apostle Paul held a different view—he made a clear distinction between the nation Israel and the newly inaugurated church of Jesus.[29] He explained that God's "mystery," hidden for ages, is the church.[30] Contained in that mystery is the truth that salvation would extend beyond the Jews to Gentiles. Further, this new church would be made up of both groups. Romans 11 reveals that Gentiles were not originally a part of God's covenant promise of salvation, but that they were later "grafted in."[31] Abraham is pictured as the "root" of the olive tree. The Jewish nation are branches which have been "broken off" because of their disobedience, and the Gentiles are the "wild olive" branches "grafted in" so that they might enjoy the "rich root" (salvation) of the olive tree (Romans 11:13-21).

This is where we have to be clear, so as to avoid confusion. *Within the church*, it is true that there is "neither Jew nor Greek…for you are all one in Christ Jesus" (Galatians 3:28-29). The cross of Jesus tears down the wall that formerly divided the two, and thus God's mystery, the church, is revealed (Ephesians 2:11-18). Paul sees the fulfillment of Genesis 12:3 ("in you all the families of the earth will be blessed") in the Gentiles' salvation (Galatians 3:8-9). We are all one in Him, regardless of nationality, ethnicity, or social status (Colossians 3:11). The spiritual benefit of salvation prophesied in the Abrahamic covenant applies to *all* who trust in Jesus Christ.

So salvation is prophesied in the Abrahamic covenant for both Jew and Gentile. And yet within that same covenant are promises made to the *nation* Israel, promises that have yet to see their ultimate, literal fulfillment.

You may be wondering why I'm taking the time to highlight this distinction. I mean, does it really even matter or make a difference?

Yes, and here's why: Paul said that God's dealings with Israel's disobedience resulted in a "partial hardening…until the fullness of the Gentiles has come in; and so all Israel will be saved" (Romans 11:25-26). In other words, God has placed the nation Israel "on hold" while He gathers His Son's bride (the church) for salvation. However, this hardening of Israel is both partial and temporary. It won't last forever. When all the Gentiles who have been appointed for salvation come to faith, the church will be raptured, and God will once again turn His attention back to the nation Israel, as outlined in Daniel and Revelation. And why would He bother to return to the Jewish people after all these years? Because, as Paul further explained, "the gifts and the calling of God are *irrevocable*."[32] In other words, God never breaks an unconditional promise. He has bound Himself by His own word and character to the covenant He made with Abraham. He could no more break it than He could break any promise He has made to us as His blood-bought children.

Lessons for Last-Days Believers

So what can we learn from all this? What do the ancients teach us? To recap, we have seen that America has strong Christian roots. Our country's beginnings, both colonial and governmental, were rooted in a strong biblical influence. Because of this, Americans have been a fortunate people, enjoying the benefits afforded to us by such a founding. Even so, this country was not founded as a theocracy or a church state. Nations cannot be "Christian."

We have also learned that America is not the "new Israel," nor is our country the "Promised Land." *Israel* is Israel. And the land God swore to give Abraham and his descendants forever is located in the Middle East, not between Canada and Mexico.

So where does that leave us? What can we say about God's relationship to America and other Gentile nations, from biblical times until now?

Let's look at it in terms of four principles:

Principle 1—God Judges Nations Based on Their Moral Conscience and National Character

I will address this more specifically in the next chapter, but we could learn a lot from looking at the way ancient peoples and nations lived, and how God responded to them. Noah's world rejected God as creator and ruler, pursuing violence and depravity. As a result of this, God, in His righteousness destroyed them. But it's not just entire civilizations He has dealt with in this way. He has also chosen to annihilate individual cities due to their abhorrent sin.[33] His judgment has fallen on nations as well.[34] He has even brought illness and death to government officials whose arrogance kept them from acknowledging Him.[35]

Principle 2—*God Judges Nations Based on Their Treatment of Israel*

What does the Abrahamic covenant teach us about God's relationship to America? We cannot simply ignore the covenant God made with Abraham, as it is perpetually applicable to all countries throughout time and on into the last days. Every nation that deals unjustly with Israel will ultimately suffer the fate of past countries and peoples who did the same. History shows this to be true. Upon establishing His covenant with Abraham, God declared that His dealings with the nations would be *dependent upon their treatment of His covenant people, Israel*. Because this is part of an everlasting, unconditional covenant, it is therefore still in effect today. This means America's relations and dealings with Israel directly impacts God's favor or judgment upon us as a nation.

God's prophecy made through Isaiah concerning Babylon is a chilling reminder of His pledge to curse those nations who mistreat Israel:

> I was angry with my people
>   and desecrated my inheritance;
> I gave them into your hand,
>   and you showed them no mercy.
> Even on the aged
>   you laid a very heavy yoke.
> You said, "I am forever—
>   the eternal queen!"
> But you did not consider these things
>   or reflect on what might happen.
> Now then, listen, you lover of pleasure,
>   lounging in your security
>   and saying to yourself,

'I am, and there is none besides me.
I will never be a widow
    or suffer the loss of children.'
Both of these will overtake you
    in a moment, on a single day:
    loss of children and widowhood.
They will come upon you in full measure,
    in spite of your many sorceries
    and all your potent spells.
You have trusted in your wickedness
    and have said, "No one sees me."
Your wisdom and knowledge mislead you
    when you say to yourself,
"I am, and there is none besides me."
Disaster will come upon you,
    and you will not know how to conjure it away.
A calamity will fall upon you
    that you cannot ward off with a ransom;
    a catastrophe you cannot foresee
    will suddenly come upon you.[36]

How can we expect a different fate if we turn our back on Israel?

Principle 3—God Did Not Withhold Judgment from His Own People, Israel

If this is true, why then would a godless Gentile nation like ours be spared judgment? When the people of Israel disobeyed, God disciplined them, sometimes by sending other nations to oppress, conquer, or subjugate them.[37] If He does this with His own covenant people, what will He do with those countries who openly and proudly reject and defy Him?

Principle 4—God's Judgment Fell on Jesus at the Cross So That All the Nations Could Be Blessed

The Bible is the story of the redemption of mankind through the Jewish Messiah, and we are the beneficiaries of that story. And the good news of that redemption is found in the Abrahamic covenant. Since the patriarch's time, the promise of salvation was passed down through the ages. And because of the cross, the resurrection, and Pentecost, salvation spread from Jerusalem to Judea, Samaria, and the uttermost parts of the world at that time. From Asia Minor it made its way to Rome, and eventually to the rest of Europe, including England. And we already know that our first colonists were Christians from England. America's gospel heritage is a chain of faith traced back to a promise made to a nomadic pilgrim around 1900 BC. The way of life we Americans have enjoyed is a direct result of biblical ideals and principles embedded in our founding. Building upon this foundation is the gospel's positive influence on the United States throughout our history.

So now that we know all this, how can we biblically evaluate the state of our nation? Just how bad does our country have to get before God's judgment officially begins? Or has it *already* begun? Could we currently be experiencing that wrath? And if so, what does it look like?

The Road to Abandonment

The last experience of the sinner
is the horrible enslavement of the freedom he desired.

—C.S. Lewis

Ephraim is joined to idols; let him alone.

—Hosea 4:17

We learned earlier that English evangelist George Whitfield was one of the most powerful Christian figures of the eighteenth century. Wherever he travelled in colonial America, thousands would flock to hear him preach. But though his oratory skills held audiences spellbound, he was, nevertheless, a highly controversial figure. One of the reasons for this was that Whitfield simply held nothing back. He spoke bluntly about sin, sins, and salvation. Because of this, some churches refused to allow him into their pulpits. In fact, so offended were some of his listeners that, on occasion, they even hurled objects at him while he preached, including rotten eggs, stones, and even a dead cat!

That's "dead cat preaching."

This chapter qualifies under that category. Translated: What you are about to read is filterless, and will likely offend some.

Jesus's preaching often had the same effect. For example, when He described the nature of genuine salvation to His disciples, Jesus warned,

> Not everyone who says to Me, "Lord, Lord," will enter the kingdom of heaven, but he who does the will of My Father who is in heaven will enter. Many will say to Me on that day, "Lord, Lord, did we not prophesy in Your name, and in Your name cast out demons, and in Your name perform many miracles?" And then I will declare to them, "I never knew you; depart from Me, you who practice lawlessness" (Matthew 7:21-23).

These words are clearly offensive to those who believe all religions lead to heaven. But they are also authoritative, as Jesus is God.[1] According to Him, *knowing God* is the authenticating trademark of every true believer. Being religious, being good, trying hard, or joining a church won't cut it. But *knowing God* will. Later, Jesus would define the essence of eternal life in the same way…knowing God.[2] And yet many of today's Christians struggle to articulate what this phrase actually means. Beyond an elementary understanding of God as a loving Father, Jesus as a friend to sinners, the importance of living a good life, and serving others, their knowledge of God doesn't go much deeper. Is it any surprise, then, that the average American's understanding of God is even more shallow?

Researcher George Gallop has stated, "Americans revere the Bible—but by and large, don't read it. And because they don't read it, they have become a nation of biblical illiterates."[3] Most Christians cannot name the Ten Commandments or even the books of the Bible. Further, a Barna poll found that 12 percent of Americans believe Joan of Arc was Noah's wife.[4] Another survey discovered that more than 50 percent of graduating high school seniors thought Sodom and Gomorrah were husband and wife![5]

Of course, it comes as no surprise that unbelievers would be ignorant about Scripture. But this epidemic of biblical illiteracy has also infected the church. A 2014 Lifeway Research study revealed that just "45% of those who attend church regularly read the Bible more than once a week. Eighteen percent say they don't read it at all."[6] And yet, as professing Christians, we claim a loyalty and affinity to the Word of God.

These sad realities beg a legitimate question. If those who call themselves Jesus's disciples rarely, if ever, engage the only book He ever wrote, how can they possibly know for sure it's the Jesus of the Bible they are actually following? From where do their ideas and beliefs about God, life, salvation, morality, mankind, and the end times come, if not the Bible? Tragically, a result of this widespread ignorance and lack of interaction with Scripture has produced a generation of churched youth and adults who possess only a surface knowledge of who their God is. And if they do not really know Him, what does this say about the legitimacy of their faith?

Perhaps nowhere is this lack of understanding more revealed than when the subject of God's wrath is mentioned. Granted, not your typical dinner table (or church) conversation, the subject of God's wrath is treated somewhat as *taboo*, like it's somehow God's "dark side." We don't talk about it much, in part because it feels negative. We prefer our heavenly Father to be loving, merciful, and gracious—which of course He is in abundance. His grace is truly immeasurable and indescribable. And yet, in our humanity and spiritual immaturity, our attention is more easily captured by those divine attributes that give us immediate comfort, not confusion. It's much easier to dwell on the characteristics of God that evoke feelings of tranquility, not terror. The result is that, because of the awkwardness it brings, we either downplay or avoid mention of God's wrath altogether. Preferring to think more "positively," we simply dodge talk of judgment.

But to sidestep the reality of God's wrath is just as negligent as ignoring His love. The Bible (the same Bible so many Christians neglect today) paints a portrait of a God who is just as righteous and wrathful as He is caring and compassionate. Amazingly, none of His attributes compete with one another. None of them are mutually exclusive or cancel one another out. Rather, they exist and cooperate in harmonic, holy perfection. It's important that we understand this bedrock principle so as not to think the following truths are tangential or irrelevant to our lives and country.

Understanding God's Wrath

Let's begin by asking a few key questions regarding the wrath of God:

1. Why even talk about wrath?

- It is an attribute of God. It's who He is, a wrathful God.

- The Bible talks about God's wrath, therefore so should we.

- The prospect and reality of wrath is a healthy deterrent to sin.

- Truth about divine judgment serves as a call to salvation and a motivation to flee from the wrath to come.

2. What exactly is God's wrath?

- God's wrath can be defined as the expression of His

divine displeasure toward sin. It is the outpouring of His judgment, retribution, vengeance, and divine punishment (2 Thessalonians 1:7-8).

- Wrath is God's righteousness in action. It can be expressed actively and decisively, like a judge's gavel, or passively, over time.

3. How is God's wrath revealed?

- Creation reveals God's wrath (more about that in a moment).

- We see divine wrath toward sin poured out on Jesus at the cross.[7] During His six hours of suffering, the Father not only blasted His Son with an eternity's worth of righteous anger, but also temporarily abandoned Him.[8] And why? Because the wages of sin is *death*, or separation from God.[9]

4. What are the different manifestations of God's wrath?

Everlasting/Eternal Wrath, or Hell

Here, in a literal place of constant, conscious torment, all those who refuse the offer of salvation through Jesus will spend an uninterrupted eternity being tormented by God's wrath without opportunity for reprieve or relief (Revelation 14:9-11). In fact, all unbelievers are currently under the *sentence* of this impending wrath.[10]

End-Times Wrath

This refers to the unleashing of God's judgment on planet earth and its inhabitants during the coming Tribulation period (Revelation 6–19; 6:15-17). It is from this wrath that Jesus promises to deliver His bride (1 Thessalonians 1:10; 5:9; Revelation 3:10).

Catastrophic Wrath

This would be cataclysmic judgments on a nation or people, such as the global flood (Genesis 6–9) or the plagues of Egypt (Genesis 7–11).

"Harvest" Wrath

God has ordained this law of wrath as a natural consequence to sin this side of eternity. What a person, people, or nation sows is what they will also reap (Galatians 6:7-10; 2 Corinthians 9:6; Proverbs 1:31-33; 5:21-23; 22:8; Job 4:7-9; Hosea 8:1-14; 10:12-15). God says that *planting* sin in your life produces a *harvest* of consequence and judgment. These residual effects of sin may happen naturally or as a direct judgment from God.[11] Though the reaping is not always immediate, as a general rule, it does eventually occur. This principle of sowing and reaping applies positively to good actions as well.

Abandonment Wrath

This kind of judgment occurs when God releases a person or society, allowing them to go their own way without any intervention or help from heaven. In the Old Testament, God's anger burned against Israel on many occasions, provoking His discipline. But abandonment wrath was also exercised against Israel as well, albeit temporarily (Psalms 81:12; Hosea 4:17; Acts 7:38-42). Because we as Christians are His children, God has promised to never abandon us.[12] He has not, however, made this promise to Gentile nations. Typically after natural disasters occur, you can count on at least one high-profile religious figure attributing that disaster to God's judgment as punishment for sin. Meanwhile, unbelievers lament, "Why would God allow such a thing?"

But divine abandonment is not about hurricanes, earthquakes, and natural disasters. It's about God *letting go*. And so this brings us to a serious and difficult question, one of the "dead cat" variety: Has God abandoned America?

Or put another way, Are we, as a nation, currently suffering under the wrath of God?

Just what does Scripture say regarding this abandonment, including if, how, and when it happens? Are there signs indicating God has already "let go" of our country? And how would we even know if God has already abandoned America, or if He is in the process of doing so? What does that even look like? Who would know these things?

I will first tell you who *wouldn't* know. Politicians wouldn't know. Economists wouldn't know. Social workers and educators wouldn't know. And the major news outlets wouldn't have a clue. That's because all these largely traffic in news, theory, and opinion…not truth. Only those dialed in to God's Word and His wisdom would know these things.

So what does this abandonment look like? And what does it mean, from a practical standpoint, for the United States?

To adequately answer these questions, we must consult Scripture. Only then can we begin to understand the nature and exercise of divine abandonment.

The Stages of Abandonment

The apostle Paul was a brilliant thinker who possessed an unusual understanding of theology, biblical history, and practical living. He also was personally taught by Jesus and, when penning his letters, he was directly inspired by the Holy Spirit.[13] As a result, Paul's writings are an enduring source-map, enabling us to accurately discern the times, both then and now. In his epistle to the Romans, he specifically outlined the telltale signs of a civilization that has been the recipient of divine abandonment. Let's unpack the six stages of abandonment wrath as stated in Scripture:

Stage 1—Suppression of God's Revelation (Romans 1:18-20)
Paul began,

> The *wrath* of God is revealed from heaven against all ungodliness and unrighteousness of men, who *suppress the truth* in unrighteousness, because that which is known about God is *evident within them*; for God made it evident to them. For since the creation of the world His invisible attributes, His eternal power and divine nature, have been *clearly seen*, being *understood* through what has been made, so that they are without excuse.

The apostle makes a bold claim here that puts every man, woman, boy, and girl in America on notice. He contends a supreme being exists, and that every human being *instinctively* knows it. The two evidences he presents for this innate awareness are: (1) conscience, and (2) creation.[14]

Conscience is the internal testimony regarding a greater being, and it is embedded within each of us. Like a basic operating system, it comes standard with the human hard drive. This internal knowledge includes a fundamental understanding of "right vs. wrong" and is woven into the human psyche. But when that conscience becomes "seared," a person no longer acknowledges or adheres to these revealed moral standards.[15] More about how and why this happens in a moment. But our being, which is made in the image of God, includes the capacity to intuitively understand morality.

The second evidence for the existence of God is *external*, and is the witness of *creation*. The Creator has boldly and unmistakably declared His existence and nature through what has been made. The universe is like a gargantuan blinking neon sign made up of billions of smaller signs. And every one of them proclaims the wonder and majesty of God. Thus, the logic of divine revelation is both unavoidable *and* undeniable. God made humankind, giving us eyes so that we could see the expanse of creation—the earth, sky, seas, and stars. Through what has been *made*, the human mind logically concludes there must be a *maker*. The natural, rational response to being exposed to such marvelous handiwork is to be filled with wonder, awe, and worship—and to desire more knowledge about this amazing creator.[16]

However, as a nation, America has systematically removed God as the originator of life. The existence of God was once a commonly accepted truth in society. And despite the fact that an overwhelming majority of Americans still claim belief in God or a "universal spirit," the practical outworking of that professed belief is fading fast. Though our money may still give lip service to His existence, and our founding documents refer to Him as Creator, these references have become *practically* meaningless.

Concerning the origins of the universe and human life, the fairy tale of evolution has become official policy in our schools, colleges, and universities. The suggestion that scientific creationism be taught side-by-side with Darwinian theory is met with ridicule and repulsion. A student in a secular school or college who proclaims "God made the world" is likely to experience a verbal scourging and be dismissed as superstitious. The very God who set the laws of science in motion is now relegated to the realm of fantasy or science fiction.

C.S. Lewis was no stranger to the arguments of secularism and atheism. Concerning the idea that the universe simply sprang up out of nothing, he wrote,

> Supposing there was no intelligence behind the universe, no creative mind. In that case, nobody designed my brain for the purpose of thinking. It is merely that when the atoms inside my skull happen, for physical or chemical reasons, to arrange themselves in a certain way, this gives me, as a by-product, the sensation I call thought. But, if so, how can I trust my own thinking to be true? It's like upsetting a milk jug and hoping that the way it splashes itself will give you a map of London. But if I can't trust my own thinking, of course I can't trust the arguments leading to Atheism, and therefore have no reason to be an Atheist, or anything else. Unless I believe in God, I cannot believe in thought: so I can never use thought to disbelieve in God.[17]

And how long has God made His existence known to mankind? Paul said, "Since the creation of the world" (Romans 1:20). So Adam obviously knew about this. So did Noah's generation. The citizens of Sodom knew. Pharaoh knew it but refused to admit it. So did Herod and the Caesars. But wait. If all these people clearly knew of God's existence, why didn't they acknowledge Him? If all people know from creation and conscience that God exists, why then are there skeptics, agnostics, and atheists? Paul's answer is simple: They "*suppress* the truth in unrighteousness" (1:18). In other words, they attempt to bury the truth about God. And why would they do that? Obviously, they understand that acknowledging God's existence means being accountable to Him. And *that* is the last thing a person pursuing sin wants to do. And so, they engage in life's ultimate denial. Ironically, in doing so, they deny the basis and meaning of all reality, including their own. The existence of God is a real and present threat to man's sin nature.

Another reason people suppress this truth is because Satan, the "god of this world," blinds the "minds of the unbelieving so that they may not see the light of the gospel."[18]

This is why the psalmist wrote, "The fool has said in his heart, 'There is no God.'" And what would contribute to such an illogical statement? The very next phrase explains it. "They are corrupt, they have committed abominable deeds; there is no one who does good" (Psalm 14:1).

The reason anyone would utter this kind of atheistic nonsense is because their corrupt heart has led them into sinful deeds, resulting in a seared conscience. This is why there are people who can look you in the eye and, without blinking, say that God doesn't exist. Their willful suppression of the truth about God's existence has brought them to a place where *blindness* has set in. Unfortunately for them, their "confident atheism" is built on sinking sank, for it is based on a lie. Peter prophetically warned us that in the last days "mockers…following after their own lusts" would willfully ignore God's role in the creation of the world.[19]

Even so, the overwhelming evidence of God's existence and His creative work is testimony against those who would deny Him. And that is precisely why God says they are "without excuse" (Romans 1:20). In other words, they are rightfully deserving the wrath He will reveal against them. No excuse will be accepted when they stand before Him.

So there *is* a creator, a creation, and a conscience. To deny the existence of the first one results in the misunderstanding of the second, leading to the further corruption of the third. Do this, God says, and there will be consequences.

Stage 2—The Refusal to Submit to God's Rule (Romans 1:21-22)

Paul continued,

> Even though they knew God, they did not honor Him as God or give thanks, but they became futile in their speculations, and their foolish heart was darkened. Professing to be wise, they became fools,

Paul repeated the fact that people know God exists. But in spite of this knowledge, many will stubbornly refuse to give Him the honor and gratitude He rightfully deserves. Again, God's right to rule as King in the human heart is a threat to self-rule. So because mankind has rejected the most basic, self-evident truths about the one who made him and who defines reality, he launches out on an endless search for truth and meaning. But it's an exercise in futility, as he dooms himself to dead-end pursuits. Wisdom is sought, but denied him. Truth is replaced with feelings and relativism. Godless reasonings lead only to further emptiness. He attempts to discover the origin of life, but his search is fraught with groundless speculation, which in turn produces flawed conclusions. And where knowledge *is* discovered, man takes full credit for it himself.

When a society rejects the greatest and most blatant reality (God), it is then left to the finite inventions of a diseased human mind. These speculations, by virtue of the fact that they exclude God, are by definition futile. In other words, after suppressing the truth about God, you have zero chance of even accidentally stumbling on the truth about life, love, human origins, morality, or salvation. Walking in pitch darkness, you are destined to hopeless wandering.

This refusal to respond to the simple light of creation and conscience carries consequences. Those who reject the light, sentence themselves to an even deeper darkness of heart (Romans 1:21). Further, for their unwillingness to believe the truth, God will allow them to embrace a lie. What light they previously had access to will be snuffed out by God. This underscores a principle Jesus taught: The failure to respond in obedience to truth and revelation can result in a calloused heart, the removal of God's provision, and a greater susceptibility to being deceived by lies.[20] A similar deluding experience will accompany those living under Antichrist's reign during the Tribulation.[21]

There are few thoughts more frightening than the idea that God would intentionally initiate the process of letting someone go. And yet this is an expression of His judgment, and it begins the horror of abandonment wrath. Unbelievably, even then, Paul said a truth-suppressing, God-denying culture will continue to view itself with egotistical adoration. The tragic irony, of course, is that though men profess themselves to be wise, God labels them "fools" (verse 22).[22] Oh, the intoxicating deception of self, proving just how stupid sin makes us all.

Stage 3—Religion that Replaces God (Romans 1:23)

The apostle said that those who reject worship of the true God have "exchanged the glory of the incorruptible God for an image in the form of corruptible man and of birds and four-footed animals and crawling creatures."

Of the 6.9 billion people currently living on earth, 4.7 billion worship some god other than Jesus Christ.[23] These man-made religions include Islam, Buddhism, Hinduism, African religions, Chinese folk religions, Eastern mysticism, Native American traditions, and Australian aboriginal religions. Man, in his search for happiness, fulfillment, and peace, also worships counterfeit deities through the Baha'i faith, Sikhism, Shintoism, Taoism, Wicca, and Zoroastrianism. Instead of worshipping the one true God in His glory, they venerate images of humans, beasts, birds, and reptiles. From ancient Egyptian religions that worshipped birdlike deities to modern-day Hindus who revere cattle, serpent deities, and some 330 million other gods, man's darkened imagination has conjured up an untold number of false idols throughout history. Besides the obvious worship of self, many of the world's religions pay homage to other humanlike gods, honoring the creation instead of the Creator. According to Revelation, the culmination of all these false religions will converge in the latter half of the Tribulation as planet earth falls on its face to worship demons and the man of Satan's choosing.[24]

And so even though God is denied His rightful place in their lives, humanity is nevertheless compelled from within to *worship* something. Mankind cannot break free from the spiritually magnetic attraction to tap into something greater or pay homage to a god-like image or ideology. We are born worshippers. It's just how we're made. It therefore stands to reason that if we cast aside the one we were created to worship; we must then substitute something in His place. And with God out of the mix, we are left to invent new and alternative objects of worship.

What we are seeing in our world today is nothing less than global idolatry. And the more a nation turns away from God's revelation and the worship of Him, the darker the day becomes. Rationalizing truth and rejecting God as Creator, we manufacture our own religions and gods. This reality illustrates the futility of the finite mind. Searching for divinity, humanity forever wanders, never able to escape the confines of its own darkness. This is sad, because the Lord is actually nearer to the lost than they realize. As Paul proclaimed to those on Mars Hill in Athens, "They would seek God, if perhaps they might grope for Him and find Him, though He is not far from each one of us."[25]

God is not hard to find for the one who is willing to humble himself and believe.

And so, the natural consequences of rejecting revelation about God brings about a deeper darkness of the heart and an inability of the mind to discover what is real and true. But the wrath doesn't end there. In fact, it's about to get exponentially worse. At this point in the life of a person or nation, God accelerates His abandonment protocol. Darkness has already set in. And in that darkness, desire is born.

The Release of Abandonment

Stage 4—Dishonoring Desires (Romans 1:24-25)

Though America is known for her independence and freedom of choice, it is these very privileges she abuses when it comes to God. We insist on independence from His "restrictive, repressive rules," demanding our rights while asking ourselves, "What does my heart say?" More than anything, Americans resist anyone telling them what to do. Today, what is perceived as an individual *right* is considered sacred above all things, God included. Start messing with people's freedom to do what they want, and you will have a war on your hands. But again, the irony is that wanting more freedom from God directly results in a greater slavery to self and sin. As Paul further explained:

> Therefore God *gave them over* in the lusts of their hearts to impurity, so that their bodies would be dishonored among them. For they exchanged the truth of God for a lie, and worshiped and served the creature rather than the Creator, who is blessed forever. Amen (Romans 1:24-25).

The slide into abandonment takes a decidedly downward turn here. Paul chose a powerful verb to describe God's response to sin. It is, in fact, a threefold judgment that is repeated in verses 24, 26, and 28. The main verb in the original Greek text, *paradidōmi,* refers to a "handing over." It is used in the Gospels and Acts to signify being arrested or put in prison.[26] Peter used this verb when speaking of fallen angels being cast into hell by God after they sinned.[27] It is also used to refer to the Father's abandonment of Jesus at the cross, part of the penalty for bearing our sin.[28]

So why would God give people over to their own impure desires? Paul tells us in the word "therefore," which refers back to verses 18-23. A society that chooses to suppress the truth about God and creation will subsequently enter a downward spiral into futile, human speculations. Stubbornly refusing to honor God, it replaces worship of Him with false idols. And when a culture does this, it earns the consequence of divine abandonment. And just in case we missed it, Paul repeated this justification for wrath in verse 25.

The Greek word translated "lust" signifies a *strong desire,* here clearly referring to sexual desires that dishonor the body. But in what sense does sexual sin dishonor one's body? Or in what sense is it a sin against a person's own body? God considers it sin because it redefines His original intent and design of the body as it relates to sex. We dishonor our bodies by using them in ways for which they were not designed, morally speaking.

And this may be a revelation to some, but all sin is *not* the same. Shoplifting a candy bar (though clearly wrong) is not the same as sleeping with your best friend's spouse. Sexual sin is not like other sins in that it betrays the Creator's fundamental design. Its capacity for destruction has a broad scope. It is not like other sins in that it involves an intimacy that transcends other physical, emotional, or mental experiences. A sexual encounter is more than simply two bodies coming together for mutual pleasure. It is also meant to picture the *spiritual* intimacy between a male husband and his female wife.[29]

Paul certainly observed an abundance of sexual promiscuity in ancient Corinth 2000 years ago. It was part of why he urged the Corinthians to "flee immorality. Every other sin that a man commits is outside the body, but the immoral man sins against his own body."

It's why he admonished the Thessalonians, "This is the will of God, your sanctification; that is, that you abstain from sexual immorality; that each of you know how to possess his own vessel in sanctification and honor, not in lustful passion, like the Gentiles who do not know God" (1 Thessalonians 4:3-5).

We live in a society soaked in sexual sin. But this is nothing new. We are not the first culture to experience mankind's obsession with sex. However, at no time in America's history has sexual sin been so prevalent *and* promoted. And though sexuality and its accompanying desires are God-given, ours has become a culture where sexual expression and pornographic passion are portrayed as natural and even right. But the reason for this is because of the spiritual darkness that is so pervasive in our country—a darkness brought on by our national rejection of God.

In the dark, our sinful hearts deceive us into thinking everything is okay.[30] Propelled along by the current of a corrupt culture, we are unwilling to repent or cry out for help. Society embraces lies about sex while simultaneously rejecting the truth found in God's Word. Thus, our self-worship turns us both inward *and* downward. Ultimately, we become a nation whose sinful, selfish desires rule supremely. It's not difficult to document the obsession we have with lust in our country. Consider that...

- 12 percent of all Internet websites are pornographic. That's over 24 million sites.

- 77 percent of all Americans view pornography at least once a month.

- 40 million are regular visitors to those sites.

- 1 in 3 are women.

- 25 percent of all search engine requests are related to pornography.

- The most popular day of the week for viewing porn is Sunday.

- The average age a child sees his first pornographic images is now 11.[31] Some claim this average age is lowering to 9 years old. As parents cave under the pressure to provide smart phones for their children at younger ages, those children are gaining virtually unlimited access to pornographic smut. And sexual predators target such young people, posing as fellow teens or preteens.

  The images and videos that America's children are exposed to online cannot be unseen. Burned into their young minds, these images not only steal their innocence, they also promote an ungodly perspective regarding sex, gender, and romance. Sexting and sending suggestive or nude images via apps like Snapchat, KiK, and others are now common among young people.

- 93.2 percent of boys and 62.1 percent of girls will see porn before their eighteenth birthday.[32]

- The online pornography industry rakes in $10-12 billion annually.[33]

At work, at home, by the pool, at school, and in the bedroom—on our phones, tablets, and laptops—we are consuming sex in copious quantities. And though the sex buffet is always open, it is not free. In the process of our consumption, we have become a nation who has dishonored and denigrated our minds and bodies. Past generations found it more difficult to access porn, which was limited to adult periodicals. Now that content (and much worse) is literally *in the air*, and more accessible than at any other time in human history.

The scandalous pornographic novel and movie *Fifty Shades of Grey* pales in comparison to what is streamed over phones and computers every day in America. Many people justify porn habits by saying, "It's ok as long as you don't actually *do it*, right?" Not according to Jesus Christ, who declared that he who merely "looks at a woman with lust for her has already committed adultery with her in his heart" (Matthew 5:28).

So what ultimate impact is this sexual explosion having on our generation? Beyond obviously rewiring our mindset toward sex, there are emotional and relational repercussions as well. How can a man or woman possibly understand what love and intimacy really are if they have been constantly bombarded with counterfeit experiences? How can a young teenager know how to treat his eventual spouse in a society where women are not much more than objects of sexual desire?

But there is also a physical fallout. According to the Centers for Disease Control and Prevention, *half* of all sexually active people will contract an STD (Sexually Transmitted Disease) by age 25.[34] But it gets worse. It's one thing for a culture to dishonor the human body through impure sexual activity. But left to himself, man pursues even further the twisted desires of his darkened heart.

Stage 5—Degrading Passions (Romans 1:26-27)

Having rejected God, truth, and conscience, the next step in abandonment is a bent toward unnatural sexual perversion.

> *For this reason*, God gave them over to degrading passions; for their women exchanged the natural function for that which is unnatural, and in the same way also the men abandoned the natural function of the woman and burned in their desire toward one another, men with men committing indecent acts and receiving in their own persons the due penalty of their error (Romans 1:26-27).

There are several clear truths this passage teaches:

- The sin of homosexuality is a direct result of rejecting God and refusing to submit to Him (verse 18-23).[35] And it is indicative of an advanced stage of divine abandonment.

- Lesbianism is *unnatural*, and runs contrary to creation. The natural, God-ordained function of a woman is to desire a *man*, not another woman. Forsaking the *God* of nature leads to altering the *order* of nature.

- Consequently, homosexuality among men is also unnatural.

Regardless of what psychology, popular culture, political correctness, movies, social media, the US Supreme Court, or the human mind and heart may argue, it is never, under any circumstances, normal or morally right for a man to sexually desire another man. And in spite of what some claim, homosexuals are not "born that way," any more than someone is born a thief, adulterer, or murderer. It is true that we are all natural-born sinners.[36] But how each of us chooses to express our sinful heart and independence from God is up to us. Tragically, even some professedly "Christian" bloggers and authors assert that two homosexuals can experience a "holy" relationship.[37] Statements like this from religious leaders not only expose their apostasy, but also reveal a fundamental misunderstanding of who God is. Of course, homosexuals and lesbians who trust Jesus for salvation can experience God's forgiveness, salvation, and a changed life, just like any other sinner can. But apart from Him, there is no hope for any of us.

That being said, one of the signs of a nation being abandoned and judged by God is the acceptance and spread of homosexuality. When Yahweh speaks, He does not stutter. And in Genesis 16–19, He gave humanity an example of how, when a culture burns with same-sex lust toward one another, His anger burns toward them. The gay communities of Sodom and Gomorrah were engaged in gross immorality, and were summarily incinerated by the cataclysmic wrath of almighty God.[38] I understand this sounds harsh to some, but which is more tragic: a righteous God justifiably judging the wicked, or a rebellious population mocking the very God who made them?

What is worth noting is that, *on the whole*, women are not as quick to fall into moral promiscuity as men. Males are primarily motivated through visual stimuli, whereas women tend to be more relational. This is not to say that women aren't sexually tempted through sight or that men cannot be relational when it comes to sexuality. But these basic distinctions between men and women are universal due to the design and differences in the male and female brains.

This reality prompted theologian Charles Hodge to conclude, concerning lesbianism, that women are the "last to be affected in the decay of morals [in a society]; and their corruption is therefore proof that all virtue is lost."[39]

In its June 2015 decision, the US Supreme Court ruled that marital unions between lesbians and male homosexuals was officially a "right." Concerning this decision, Justice Samuel Alito remarked, "as far as I'm aware, until the end of the 20th century, there was never a nation or a culture that recognized marriage between two people of the same sex."[40]

He was right.

Though there have certainly been homosexual unions throughout time, same-sex marriage has never been widely practiced in human history, with the possible exception of one parenthetical period—the wicked generation in the days of Noah.[41] God responded by wiping those people from the face of the earth in the global flood judgment (Genesis 6–7).

Scripture bluntly declares that no homosexual will enter heaven.[42] Period. *Not one.* Even so, God deeply loves *all* homosexuals and lesbians. Jesus suffered to pay the penalty for their sin, and He rose from the dead to give them new life. They *can* be saved. *Every one of them.* The gospel is a good news message of hope, love, and redemption for anyone who calls on His name.[43] The homosexual community needs both the grace and truth that can be found only in Jesus Christ.[44] And God has rescued countless people who were formerly enslaved to this sin.

We must recognize and proclaim that truth and love are not enemies. Rather, they work together in bringing lost souls to an acknowledgment of their sin and need for salvation. Like all who have experienced salvation, homosexuals can become new creations through His saving grace and power (1 Corinthians 6:11). And though many Christians are tempted and struggle with this and many other sins, the Holy Spirit supplies the power to consistently overcome.[45]

But sin and sins separate us from God, and any nation that

promotes and celebrates this heinous sin is a country under abandonment wrath. Likewise, God's Spirit will also abandon any church or denomination who accommodates or treats this sin as normal or allowable, including those who ordain homosexuals as ministers.

Paul concludes this section of truth by highlighting the physical "penalty" associated with the promiscuity of the homosexual lifestyle, a likely reference to sexually transmitted diseases rampant among pagans in his day.[46] This comes as no real surprise, as 83 percent of homosexual men estimate they have had sex with 50 or more partners in their lifetime. Forty-three percent say they've had sex with 500 or more partners, and 28 percent with 1000 or more partners, the vast majority of these being strangers.[47]

But Paul didn't stop there. There is one final stage of divine abandonment he wanted us to understand.

Stage 6—Depraved Minds (Romans 1:28-32)

This last stage portrays a people whose collective state of mind has written God completely out of the picture. The persistent refusal to acknowledge God in their origins, their worship, and their sexuality moves God to release the parking break, propelling them toward destruction. For the third time, Paul used this phrase "God gave them over." But this time, He gave them over to a "depraved mind," compelling them to "do those things which are not proper." So what does a culture in the final stage of abandonment look like? Let's allow Paul to answer that. They are

> filled with all unrighteousness, wickedness, greed, evil; full of envy, murder, strife, deceit, malice; they are gossips, slanderers, haters of God, insolent, arrogant, boastful, inventors of evil, disobedient to parents, without understanding, untrustworthy, unloving, unmerciful (1:29-31).

I could fill this chapter with examples and statistics illustrating how America fits the above description. Instead, I encourage you to reread those verses, more slowly this time. Pause to visualize how our nation embodies these "things which are not proper." Paul is describing for us what a culture of corrupted minds looks like. The word translated "depraved" means to "fail the test," and was used to describe metals that were rejected because of impurities. A depraved mind is a spiritually diseased mind. It is impure and decayed. Because of this depravity, it no longer functions properly. It is easily deceived, embracing lies without hesitation.

And it *loves* the things that grieve the heart of God.

Spiritual decadence is a black hole, and its gravitational pull is sucking our nation into inescapable darkness…unless something supernatural happens. But meanwhile, people continue pursuing wickedness, celebrating it and giving full support to those who practice such things (verse 32). It is no longer enough for people to satisfy themselves with enjoying sin in secret. They have declared their right to pursue it openly, to justify it before the masses, and even to demand that all other Americans validate it. According to Scripture, it is these very things that ignite God's wrath (Colossians 3:5-6).

That truth should make you tremble for America.

So at what point did God let us go? Paul's inspired text reveals that this abandonment is a gradual release that occurs in stages. And yet, like birth pangs, it seems to intensify toward a dramatic climax of corruption.

How can God bless, protect, or preserve a country that promotes the very sins for which His Son Jesus died? How can any president or government leader vote to legalize and normalize that which God describes as gross immorality and an abomination? When godlessness, idolatry, immorality, and homosexuality become "official policy" in a country, what options does a holy and righteous God have?

How can anyone who believes himself or herself to be a Christian possibly support these sins when God says they are a sign of His wrath on a people? And what does it say about the biblical understanding, spiritual condition, and state of mind of any Christian who does show support?

The Implications of Divine Abandonment

By definition of God's existence, His role as Creator, and His righteous character, every person and nation is accountable to Him. He can and does abandon people and nations to themselves and to His wrath, both now and in eternity.[48] In fact, He must do this, or else He would betray His own character. The Lord is patient, but not to the denial of His righteousness.

Now, is this earthly abandonment temporary, or permanent?

As noted earlier, Christians have the assurance that God will never abandon His own children.[49] However, He does not make this same promise to Gentile nations.[50] These compelling truths from Romans are like tornado sirens or fire alarms. And they've been sounding for decades. However, America has been too preoccupied by other things to notice. And how has the church allowed such evil to continue and prosper? Have we been lulled to sleep by the complacency and prosperity of our own Christianity? Have we failed to be in God's Word enough to have our senses "trained to discern good and evil"?[51]

Like sirens alerting us to impending disaster, we shouldn't resist these alarming truths. Rather, we should be awakened by them. And be grateful for them.

Without God and His principles guiding our country, there is nowhere for America to go but down. We cannot achieve or maintain moral altitude apart from Him. We have no power to restrain sin, sustain civility, maintain human dignity, or preserve liberty. Just look around. We are rapidly descending in a spiritual and moral freefall. We're in a nosedive, losing altitude fast. Racing at the speed of sin toward impact, we are on a collision course with the consequences of our rejection of God and embracing sin.

A Right Response to Imminent Danger

I worked with teenagers and their families for many years. Though the vast majority of my experiences were positive, I also dealt with my share of rebellious kids, runaways, drug and alcohol abuse, sexual promiscuity, teen pregnancy, suicide attempts, arrests, and a host of other struggles and sins. Many of these teenagers came to their senses and returned to their God and families.

Some did not.

One of the saddest moments a minister can experience is when he has to counsel a parent to "let go." It's in the heart of every mom and dad to do everything within their power to help their children when they stray or sin. But when a person is determined to do their own thing despite repeated pleas and warnings, when help offered is consistently and vehemently refused, then the time comes when nothing more can be done—nothing except to let go.

When a parent's presence, authority, and influence are no longer sufficient or effective, then sin and life consequence become the teachers. Parents have to pull back, and sometimes *out* of the picture. And all they can do is pray, love from a distance, and hope for the best.

Has God spoken to America? Yes. In the same way He has spoken to every other Gentile nation on earth—through creation; conscience; Scripture; His Son's life, death, and resurrection; and through His ambassadors, pastors, spiritual leaders, and disciples. Through these instruments, America has been told how she can be rescued and redeemed. We have become the most gospel-saturated country on the planet, and what do we have to show for it? God has indeed spoken. But have we listened?

Collectively, we have voted God out of our politics, our government, our educational system, and our marketplace. We have wished Him gone, and He has responded.

"Wish granted."

This truth ought to strike fear in the heart of a nation, reverberating from New York to Los Angeles. It should shake us to our knees. Instead, it only fuels more celebration.

What is happening in America is happening all over the world. Because of our Christian heritage, we may have postponed our demise a little longer than other nations. There may be seasons of prosperity and peace. Times when smaller battles are won by good, and not evil. But make no mistake. We have arrived at a dark moment in our national destiny. In preparation for the end times and the fulfillment of Bible prophecy, man's sin has caused God to withdraw Himself and deliver the nations over to His wrath. At the same time, I believe He is also purifying His bride in preparation for the Bridegroom's return.

A holy God cannot accompany a nation like ours. Therefore, we are left to continue on our own—in the dark, led by our own desires and depraved guidance. Scripture indicates that we are suffering under God's abandonment wrath.

So how do we respond to this reality of judgment? What do we do? Are we at a point of no return? Will God send a mighty revival before America's final heartbeat? Or will He allow us to slowly die before we completely implode from within? What are our options here? Here are seven responses about which we should ponder and pray:

1. We can deny America's spiritual downfall, and instead claim that we're actually getting better. Why would God

ever shed His grace *and* wrath on a great nation like ours?

2. We can downgrade God's wrath, minimizing it by saying, "He may not be pleased, but He's still on our side."

3. We could argue that Paul was simply overreacting to his culture, and the idea of God "abandoning America" is a similar knee-jerk response. This perspective is nothing more than a prophetic tirade and sensationalism, designed only to sell books.

4. We could claim that abandonment wrath applies only to individuals and not nations.

5. We could argue that divine abandonment presupposes America was once close to God. And because God has no covenant relationship with Gentile nations, the concept doesn't apply to our country.

6. We could say with confidence that God has judged both nations and peoples with abandonment. His wrath is real and can be experienced in the now and not just in eternity. But whether He has judged America is "a matter of one's opinion."

7. We could say that America does indeed qualify for abandonment—that we are truly a post-Christian nation. Though not as wicked as we *can* be, we are nevertheless a godless country. We are currently under judgment and headed for even more condemnation.

So can our nation be spared? Or have we remained all these years because of the righteous remnant who live in America? We know from Scripture that God is patient concerning sinners and nations, but there comes a point in the journey away from Him where contact is lost. He times His judgments with the "completion" of a nation's sin, meaning He delays retribution until a country's sins have reached a level set by heaven.[52] In other words, a nation arrives at a place where its denial, decadence, and depravity justifies divine, national judgment and abandonment.

And I fear that this country may have long since crossed that threshold.

5

AMERICA'S HOLOCAUST

They even sacrificed their sons and their daughters to the demons,
and shed innocent blood, the blood of their sons and their daughters,
whom they sacrificed to the idols of Canaan;
And the land was polluted with the blood.

—PSALM 106:37-38

On January 20, 1942, a villa located just outside Berlin played host to a sinister gathering. Present at this meeting were 15 of Germany's highest-ranking Nazi Party and government leaders. What brought them all together to this clandestine conclave was a directive originating from the Fuhrer himself, Adolf Hitler. Their stated objective was to discuss and implement what they had dubbed the "Final Solution to the Jewish Question."

At this meeting was SS General Reinhard Heydrich, one of *Reichsführer-SS* Heinrich Himmler's top deputies. Six months earlier, Hitler had given Himmler the responsibility of eliminating any and all perceived threats to German expansion and rule. Shortly following this, on July 31, 1941, General Heydrich was authorized to begin preparations for a "complete solution to the Jewish question."

One of the first steps in their plan was to organize mobile killing units (called Einsatzgruppen), which were comprised of deputized SS soldiers and German police. Their job was to murder anyone considered to be racial or political enemies of the Vaterland (Fatherland). In late September of 1941, a deployment of these men massmurdered 33,771 Kiev Jews in a ravine called Babi Yar. But this "Ravine of No Return" would prove to be just the beginning. However, due to the severe psychological effects these grisly murders were having on the soldiers (apparently it's not natural for humans to kill innocent people), additional methods of execution were developed. One result was a mobile gas chamber mounted atop the chassis of a truck. After leading the victims on board, the door was shut and locked, whereupon carbon monoxide from the truck's exhaust was piped in, killing everyone inside.

In less than two years, Germany's killing squads mercilessly slaughtered more than a million Soviet Jews, political partisans, Gypsies, and disabled persons. But even with these additional measures, they couldn't murder fast enough. And so concentration (labor) camps were built, employing permanent centers to facilitate the murder of vast numbers of Jews. By the war's end in 1945, six million Jewish men, women, and children had taken their last breaths inside gas chambers disguised as shower facilities. Others died at the hands of Nazi doctors, having been used as human guinea pigs in bizarre medical and scientific experiments. Hitler's persecution of Jews went from subtlety to savagery, creating a bloodbath across Europe and filling the air with the ashes of what once was Israel.

How any country could tolerate or follow such a demonic dictator defies all reason and decency. But hard economic times in prewar Germany set the stage for the messiah-like figure to emerge. Hitler had helped restore the economy and brought pride and patriotism back to the country.

It took the Allied Forces time to discover and expose Hitler's death camps. And when they did, the entire civilized world recoiled in horror and contempt. For how can a nation allow the unbridled slaughter of innocent people? And how can a government of anything less than barbarians issue edicts and pass laws to that effect?

Today, three-quarters of a century later, history and the world rightfully responds with disdain and disgust at the mere mention of the name *Hitler*. And for its war atrocities, Nazi Germany became a permanent stain on humanity's record.

And yet in a strange and sick twist of history, what Germany did to the Jews is being done in America (along with 96 percent of the world's countries). It is being done to another group of people precious to God's heart.[1]

The unborn.

The practice of abortion is the greatest human injustice in the world today. It is the ultimate devaluation of life. And in the course of just one generation, it has become America's national sin and shame. Yet despite this, we continue applauding, funding, and defending it.

The Issue is Not *Tissue*

Abortion is a hotly contested issue in post-Christian America. It's divisive, polarizing people of all races, religions, and walks of life. But is this perpetual slaughter of the innocent really any different from other national sins? And if so, in what way? Where did it come from? Why do we do it? And what effect has it had on our national conscience? Why are we as a people deaf and immune to the cries of the unborn? Why have we become immune to their pain? How is this unconscionable mass murder related to Satan's hatred of God, humanity, and family? How long can heaven tolerate a country that allows such unthinkable horrors? Can anything be done? Or is it too late to turn the tide? Have we irreversibly crossed the line here?

What will a holy and just God do to a nation who, out of mere inconvenience, slaughters their own young?

Some, of course, see abortion as only a political issue, pitting Democrats versus Republicans, liberals against conservatives. Sadly, the official Democratic Party platform "strongly and unequivocally" supports Roe v. Wade, while Republicans, at least officially, oppose government funding of abortion, though in recent decades many Republican leaders have weakened in their position on abortion. To the public, one's position on the issue often appears as nothing more than a strategy to secure votes.

Others identify abortion as a women's rights issue, arguing it's a constitutional matter. In the most famous landmark abortion rights case, lawyers for the plaintiff used the Fourteenth Amendment as their weapon of choice (the same amendment that granted citizenship to former slaves and equal protection under the law), making abortion a constitutional "right to privacy" issue for a woman.

Since that ruling on January 22, 1973, mothers have been awarded the macabre "right" to end their children's lives. Part of pagan thinking in America's judicial branch is that women have an absolute "right" over their own body. This logically makes sense if you conclude (as a nation and as an individual) that there is no God who made us, a conclusion the Bible flatly contradicts.[2] For if God *does* exist, then every person has a moral obligation to submit to His standards governing the treatment of the body.

Besides, even if one believes it's "your body," that doesn't mean you should slash and cut yourself, or commit suicide (unless, of course, there really is no God, in which case a person's life would have no real value). The other problem with abortion being a women's rights issue is that those who take this stance conveniently deny the right for *unborn* females to control *their* own bodies. So much for empowering women.

Then there's abortion from a women's health care/reproductive rights perspective. This argument states that access to abortion falls under the larger umbrella of *medical* care to which all women are entitled. In other words, a woman's "reproductive rights" means she is somehow owed a choice on whether or not to end her baby's life because abortion is "health care," just as much as going to the doctor to treat a virus, sore throat, sprained ankle, or a tumorous growth. These "reproductive rights" entitle a woman to choose both the time and execution method of her baby.

But this argument falls on its face because, while a woman's body is certainly *affected* by pregnancy, the body she actually ends up killing doesn't belong to her at all. If abortion was a decision only about a woman's body, then the woman would die in the procedure (which of course she doesn't). Instead, someone *else's* body is affected and destroyed. Abortion kills the *baby's* body, not the mother's. The mother chooses death for the child, who is denied any chance to vote on the issue. Before breathing his first breath, he is robbed of any chance at life beyond the womb.

Another way the health care industry (an oxymoronic phrase in this case) suppresses the murder element in abortion is by carefully rewording the relevant terminology. By softening the grisly language of abortion, they seek to sterilize and generalize the conversation. Hitler never publicly advertised a campaign to "Annihilate Those Inferior Jews!" Rather, he sold it to his leadership as a "Final Solution" for the good of the Third Reich (Great German Realm).

Abortion advocates do the same, employing phrases like *safe procedure* and *best medical care*. But this procedure isn't *safe* or *best* for the child, is it? And it certainly doesn't constitute *care*. Planned Parenthood uses words like *fetus* in place of *baby*, and *tissue* instead of *child*. They don't say, "We're going to inject you with chemicals so your baby will burn alive inside you." Instead, they counsel the mother, explaining, "You'll be given some medication to help the procedure." Instead of referring to the death of the baby, they call it "termination of the pregnancy." Clinic employees wear lab coats and carry clipboards, giving the impression they are there to help. Mothers are encouraged to "make a decision that's right for *you*." But based on what system of morality? When there is no objective standard (or divine standard), morality becomes relative, and varies greatly from person to person. Hence, what's right for *you*. Again, the focus is on self, not the helpless, dependent child inside the womb.

Abortion certainly involves the mother, but it does not impact the mother's ability to continue living. Not so for the child. Abortion advocates claim that it's a decision made by a woman, for a woman. This, in effect, exalts personal choice to a blasphemous level, turning women into goddesses who sacrifice their children on the altar of self. And they become the very murderers we saw in Romans 1.

In the United States, you risk much if you attempt to deny a woman her "right" to destroy the life growing inside her. The irony here is that we no longer protect the innocent from the one person whose God-ordained task it is to protect him and birth him into the world. The female womb, brilliantly designed by the Creator to nourish and shelter, is transformed into a death chamber, effectually making a mother's body no different than the gas chambers and crematoriums used in such places as Auschwitz and Dachau. How sad that a baby should get a funeral before he or she gets a birthday.

So if you still think that abortion is only about politics, women's rights, or health care, then you have succumbed to the conforming pressure of a world gone mad.[3] Abortion is first and foremost a spiritual and moral issue. And unless we address it as such, it will continue to bounce around in a never-ending false narrative of health care, women's rights, and politics.

The Valley of Slaughter

Murdering the unborn is not new. It's not something invented by feminists or Democrats. In fact, the history of abortion traces back thousands of years.

The earliest known record of abortion is found in the Ebers Papyrus (ca. 1550 BCE), an ancient Egyptian medical document. The Ebers Papyrus indicates an abortion could be induced by using a plant-fiber tampon covered with honey and crushed dates.[4] Subsequently, other herbal abortion-inducing drugs were used, including silphium, a popular medicinal plant of the ancient world (now extinct), and pennyroyal, a toxic species of mint used to cause uterine contractions.[5]

The ancient Chinese used mercury to induce abortions, and the killing of preborn babies was commonplace in Rome.[6] So too was infanticide for any child under three unless they were "maimed or monstrous from their very birth."[7] Even so, infanticide became a fairly common practice, in which Seneca (a Roman philosopher, statesman, and advisor to Nero) compared "unnatural progeny" to the killing of mad dogs, savage ox, and sickly sheep, and allowing for the drowning of "children who at birth are weakly and abnormal."[8]

Pliny the Elder (AD 23–79) wrote that "man is the only animal that repents of his first embraces" (or killing a child produced from the "embrace" of sexual relations). How odd, that of all creation, the most intelligent species on earth would regret the creation of life.

In an attempt to justify today's practices, abortion rights activists claim, "Over several centuries and in different cultures, there is a *rich history* of women helping each other to abort."[9]

A history, perhaps. However, for the person who believes life begins at conception, destroying the innocent is anything but "rich."

In 1921, a large cemetery of sacrificed infants was discovered at Carthage. Hundreds of burial urns containing cremated infant bones (mostly newborns) were uncovered in this cemetery.[10] A practice believed to have originated in Phoenicia, child sacrifice was fairly common in biblical times.

Found on these burial monuments were the names or symbols of the goddess Tanit, the chief Phoenician female deity, and her spouse, Ba'al Hammon. Burial inscriptions read, "To our lady, to Tanit, the face of Ba'al and to our lord, to Ba'al Hammon."[11]

Regular sacrifices of infants and children were made to these dual deities. Tanit was considered the "*mother* goddess," who was invoked for *fertility* blessings. Oh, the irony.

Plutarch wrote that the area immediately surrounding the statue of Tanit was filled with flute players and individuals beating drums. They were placed there to prevent children's horror-filled cries from being heard by the general public while being slaughtered.[12]

Up to 20,000 burial urns have now been uncovered at Carthage, all incinerated simply to appease a female deity. Today, instead of paying homage to one female goddess, we confer that godlike status to all woman.

Ancient Israel was repeatedly warned by God not to adopt the despicable practices of the Canaanites. Prior to entering the Promised Land, God warned the people of Israel not to assimilate Canaanite culture into their own and imitate their demonic and barbaric practices. But they refused to heed these warnings, and the Lord eventually brought judgment upon them.[13]

One of those Canaanite gods was Molech (1 Kings 11:5-7), who was portrayed as a half-man, half-bull creature. Some 400 years after the Israelites entered the land, Solomon would pay homage to Molech, his heart having been turned away from his God by his pagan wives. For this idolatrous worship, his kingdom was torn from him.[14] The high place Solomon built for Molech was located on what later became known as the Mount of Olives.[15]

Sad, as God's prior instruction to Israel regarding these pagan practices had been clear and direct:

> Do not give any of your children to be sacrificed to Molek, for you must not profane the name of your God. I am the LORD (Leviticus 18:21 NIV).

> Any Israelite or any foreigner residing in Israel who sacrifices any of his children to Molek is to be put to death. The members of the community are to stone him. I myself will set my face against him and will cut him off from his people; for by sacrificing his children to Molek, he has defiled my sanctuary and profaned my holy name. If the members of the community close their eyes when that man sacrifices one of his children to Molek and if they fail to put him to death, I myself will set my face against him and his family and will cut off from their people together with all who follow him in prostituting themselves to Molek (Leviticus 20:1-5 NIV).

Clearly, killing your children by sacrificing them to a demon god was considered evil by Yahweh, as the judgment administered for such a sin was death by stoning. Further, God declared that He would turn against those who did this. If the people failed to follow through with executing the sentence, God Himself would ensure that he, and all who participated in the same sin, would suffer the same judgment.

Generations passed following the conquest, long after Solomon's reign, and God's people still succumbed to practicing child sacrifice. God said the place where these detestable sacrifices were carried out would one day be called "the Valley of Slaughter."[16] It is because of this and other sins that the Lord came to describe Judah as a nation that "did not obey the voice of the LORD their God or accept correction; truth has perished and has been cut off from their mouth" (Jeremiah 7:28). Following the Babylonian Captivity, this valley of Hinnom (Greek, *Gehenna*) in Jesus's day became a place for burning garbage and the bodies of executed criminals.[17] Christ likely referred to this, along with this location's ancient reputation for child sacrifice, when describing the perpetual, furious fire of God (i.e. hell), where those who reject Him will burn in torment for eternity.[18]

In Leviticus 18, the prohibition against child sacrifice is, oddly enough, found in the midst of references to *sexual* sins. This is possibly due to the fact that these were all practices associated with Canaanite religion. But it could also be because every one of these sins threatens the sanctity of the family, God's first and foundational institution and the bedrock of human civilization. But the progression of sins in this passage is more than mere coincidence. Like Romans 1, Leviticus 18 outlines a *sequence* of sins that prompted God to deliver divine judgment.

And what were some of the sins (called "abominations") that brought condemnation to the inhabitants of Canaan? Incest (18:6-17), adultery (verses 18-20), child sacrifice (verse 21), homosexuality (verse 22), and bestiality (verse 23).

In this same passage, God warned His people not to "defile yourselves by any of these things," adding that this is what defiles the land and brings His judgment (verses 24-25). As with the "sins of the Amorites," fullness of sin brings fullness of wrath.

So are there any appropriate parallels between ancient Canaanite practices, the people of Israel, child sacrifice, and *us*? To begin with, taking the life of a child, whether in the womb or outside of it, is murder. Unless this truth is acknowledged and accepted, nothing about abortion makes sense from a morality standpoint. If there is no God, abortion is neither right nor wrong. Without a moral Lawgiver, there cannot be any absolute morality attached to the act. It's just something we do as humans. However, the God of Scripture does exist, and there is a mandate against abortion. Fundamentally, there is no difference between euthanizing a newly born child and slaughtering that same baby minutes earlier while still in her mother's womb. Thousands of years ago, the Canaanites sacrificed newborn infants before a statue of Molech, while today we sacrifice preborn infants in abortion clinics and hospitals. Both are brutal executions. One satisfies the demands of a demon god, while the other appeases the desires of a mother.

Second, God does not allow nations who practice such atrocities to escape the inevitable consequences of judgment. Collectively, they receive divine retribution—either by conquest, collapsing from within, or through experiencing some form of supernatural visitation and judgment.

Third, as a nation, Israel was in a special covenantal relationship with Yahweh. As such, she and her leaders (both governmental and spiritual) were responsible to follow His ways and avoid the customs and morals of the pagan nations who dwelled nearby. Though I see a clear distinction between national Israel and the church, Christians nevertheless are called to the same principle of moral separation. We are not to remove ourselves from culture, but we are called to avoid being influenced by certain ungodly values and cultural practices. A professing believer in Jesus does not have to think twice regarding the immorality of abortion. The fact that some do is an indication that worldly thinking has embedded itself in their minds, and it could be an indication of something even worse.[19]

Fast-forwarding to the first century, human sacrifice was rare in Rome, though abortion was still practiced. Because of this, as early as the second century, Jesus's church began addressing the subject. In the Didache (a compilation of the 12 apostles' teaching, AD 150), we find the following passage:

> The second commandment of the teaching: You shall not murder. You shall not commit adultery. You shall not seduce boys. You shall not commit fornication. You shall not steal. You shall not practice magic. You shall not use potions. *You shall not procure [an] abortion, nor destroy a newborn child* (Didache 2:1).

In AD 170, Mark Felix, a Christian lawyer, wrote, "There are some women among you who by drinking special potions extinguish the life of the future human in their very bowels, thus committing *murder* before they even give birth."[20]

The early Christians in the Roman Empire were accused of being atheists (for not acknowledging Roman gods), carrying on incestuous relationships (because of the Christian command for "brothers and sisters" to "love one another"), and cannibalism (eating and drinking the "body and blood" of Jesus during communion). In defense of his Christian brothers and sisters, apologist and church father Athenagoras wrote in AD 177,

> What man of sound mind, therefore, will affirm, while such is our character, that we are murderers?...When we say that those women who use drugs to bring on abortion commit murder, and will have to give an account to God for the abortion, on what principle should we commit murder? For it does not belong to the same person to regard the very fetus in the womb as a created being, and therefore an object of God's care, and when

it has passed into life, to kill it; and not to expose an infant, because those who expose them are chargeable with child-murder, and on the other hand, when it has been reared to destroy it.[21]

Another early church leader wrote, "Christians marry, like everyone else, and they beget children, but they do not cast out their offspring."[22]

In fact, throughout the first several hundred years of church history, many of the church fathers condemned abortion and infanticide.[23]

Constitutional Rights and Moral Wrongs

Today, like ancient Rome and the barbaric nations that preceded them, it is no surprise that many still vehemently argue for the moral and legal right to abort babies. But why? What is their rationale? Why, according to advocates for abortion, should a woman have the "right to choose"?

Planned Parenthood claims that "3 out of 10 women in the U.S. have an abortion by the time they are 45 years old."[24] Even more disturbing is that, according to research, half (50 percent) of all women in the United States will have an abortion in their lifetime. But why? Here are some of the most often-used reasons women give for choosing to have an abortion:

- I am not ready to become a parent (21 percent).

- I cannot afford a baby (21 percent).

- I am pressured by parents, partner, or husband (1.5 percent).

- I don't want to be a single parent (12 percent).

- I don't want anyone to know I have had sex or that I am pregnant (1 percent).

- I already have too many children (19 percent).

- I have (or the fetus has) a health problem (6 percent).

- I was a victim of rape or incest (1 percent).[25]

- I am concerned about how having a baby will change my life and future plans (16 percent).

- Various other reasons (1.5 percent).[26]

But at the heart of the abortion debate is a fundamental forgotten (or ignored) question: Is an unborn baby human simply a "*potential* human" or an actual one? Is it life or not? Failed presidential candidate Hillary Clinton famously doubled down on her assertion that an "unborn person" has no constitutional rights, and therefore no fundamental right to live.[27] Her comment angered both sides of the abortion debate. While effectively declaring all unborn children as somehow *subhuman*, abortion rights activists were outraged that she used the word *person* (a term that legally equates to certain protections and inalienable rights) instead of *fetus*.

Prolife Responses to Prochoice Arguments

While a student at Dallas Theological Seminary, I had the privilege of studying under some of our generation's greatest biblical scholars, theologians, linguists, and apologists. One of them was Dr. Norman Geisler. Then, as now, the prochoice camp continues to assemble an arsenal of arguments with which to justify the practice of abortion. Dr. Geisler's response was to confront these arguments head on using nothing more than science and logic. With Geisler's approach in mind, here are 12 arguments that attempt to justify abortion, and his accompanying responses.

1. *"No one knows when human life begins."*

Response: If no one knows when life begins, then it *might* begin at conception, right? And if it does, then abortion is murder. Can we really justify killing what *could* be a human being? Should we shoot at a moving object in the woods if we are not sure whether or not it is human? Then neither should we kill babies if we are not sure they are not human.

Actually, we do know when human life begins. It begins at conception. A sperm, with just its 23 chromosomes, is not a human being; nor is an ovum, with its 23 chromosomes. But when they unite into one entity with 46 chromosomes, the result is a human being. This is a medical fact.

2. *"The mother has the right to control her own body."*

Response: First, a baby is not *part* of its mother's body. It is an individual human being, with its own separate body. To be sure, the mother is "feeding" the unborn baby, but does a mother have the right to stop feeding her baby *after* it is born? This would be murder by starvation, and to cut off the source of life for a preborn baby is also a morally culpable act.

Second, even if the unborn baby were part of its mother's body, does she have a right to do *anything* she wants to her own body?

3. *"The unborn baby is not really human until it is born."*

Response: If a baby is not human before it is born, then what is it? It is not a mineral or a vegetable. It is not an animal such as a dog or a monkey, or an animal at all. It is a human being. Cows give birth to cows; horses give birth to horses. No medical person has any difficulty identifying an unborn dog as a dog, or an unborn pig as a pig. Why should there be any question about an unborn human?

Does this argument mean babies are human only when they

change their location and move outside the womb? Since when does *where* one lives determine one's humanity? The difference between babies who are born and those who are unborn is not their essential nature; rather, it is simply a matter of size and location.

4. *"Unborn babies are not conscious beings."*

Response: This objection assumes that one must have consciousness in order to be human. But if consciousness determines humanness, then sleeping adults are not human. And if consciousness is the test for humanness, then whenever people lapse into a coma, they instantly lose their humanity. The logical conclusion from this reasoning is that it would never be considered murder to kill an unconscious person. Therefore, all a killer needs to do is to simply knock out his victim before shooting the person!

Actually, babies in the womb *are* conscious. By four to six weeks after conception, they have their own brain waves, which they will keep for life. If the absence of a brain wave is considered a sign of death, why, then, is the presence of a brain wave not considered a sign of life?

5. *"Every child has a right to a meaningful life."*

Response: What do you consider to be the criteria for a "meaningful life," and who decides whether or not a life is meaningful? This kind of reasoning leads to aborting Down syndrome children or any unborn who have a defect of some kind or another.

The logic used by abortionists leads inevitably to infanticide and euthanasia.

6. *"It is better to have an aborted child than to have an abused one."*

Response: This assumes that delivering unwanted babies automatically leads to abuse. Statistics show just the opposite. Child abuse cases have actually *increased* as the number of abortions has gone up. Apparently the disregard for human life reflected in the acceptance of abortion is extended from the prebirth to the postbirth attitude toward offspring.

Also, the objection wrongly assumes that abortion itself is not abuse. In reality, abortion is one of the worst abuses that can possibly be inflicted on a human being.

7. *"We cannot legislate morality."*

Response: If this is so, then we should get rid of all the legislated morality we now have on the books. We could start by rescinding our prohibitions against murder, cruelty, theft, child abuse, incest, and rape. All of these are cases of morals being legislated. It is, in fact, impossible (and undesirable) to avoid legislating morality.

8. *"No mentally retarded child should be brought into the world."*

Response: No organization of parents with mentally retarded children has endorsed abortion on demand. Families with Down syndrome children regard them with real joy because of their children's capacity for unfeigned love.

Mentally challenged children are still human, and killing them is killing humans. Just because the unborn are smaller (and defenseless) does not justify killing them. Again, the logic by which abortionists justify therapeutic abortions would also justify infanticide.

9. *"Why should a rape victim be forced to bear a child she did not will to have?"*

Response: Rape is one of the worst indignities a person can suffer, and one must have great compassion for rape victims. However, keep in mind that there is no way to become "unraped." Becoming "unpregnant" (via abortion) cannot make one "unraped." Second, justice cannot be obtained for the rape victim by punishing the unborn baby who resulted from the rape.

Two wrongs do not make a right. It doesn't help a mother to burden her with the guilt of a murder on top of the indignity of being raped.

10. *"People are going to have abortions anyway, so we might as well legalize them."*

Response: Should we also legalize rape and child abuse, since people are going to carry out these deeds as well? Should we add incest and cruelty to the legal list because people persist in doing them? This argument is ludicrous. Legalizing an evil never makes it morally right.

11. *"We should never project our morality on others."*

Response: If this is so, then why are abortionists projecting their morality on the unborn? They are saying, in effect, "It is my moral belief that you should not live." In the case of abortion, *projecting morality* is exactly what we need because it is better to project morality than to project immorality. If those who are able to protect the innocent in this way do not do so, then who will?

12. *"No unwanted baby should ever be born."*

Response: This makes an assumption that an unwanted conception will automatically result in an unwanted baby. Many an unpleasantly surprised mother changes her mind once the initial shock of her unplanned pregnancy wears off and she has a chance to reflect more calmly on the situation. And even more of these reluctant mothers feel different once their babies are born.

Further, even if the mother does not want to keep the baby, there are many mothers who are unable to have children and yet desperately want them. In fact, there are at present more people who want children than there are children to want.

Just because a mother does not want a baby does not mean she has a right to kill it. We should never place our *wishes* ahead of others' *rights*, especially their right to life itself.[28] A person's fundamental right to live trumps another right to so-called "constitutional privacy."

What Happens in an Abortion?

Though most doctors today no longer swear to the Hippocratic Oath, there is a certain irony in that it includes the following vow: "I will give no deadly medicine to any one if asked, nor suggest any such counsel; and in like manner I will not give to a woman a pessary to produce abortion."[29]

Most modern medical oaths omit any reference to abortion, and are more ceremonial than binding.

So how exactly is an abortion performed? What methods are being employed today in America's "death camp clinics"? Here are the most common:

Abortion Pill—Usually taken up to 10 weeks after becoming pregnant, there are actually 2 pills given that contain 2 separate chemicals. One prompts the lining of the uterus to break down, while the other causes the uterus to empty, expelling the baby. All of this is accompanied by severe cramps and heavy bleeding. The abortion pill is about 95 percent effective.

Suction Aspiration—Also called *vacuum aspiration*, this is the most common method in use today. Mostly used during the first trimester, this method employs a powerful suction tube placed into the dilated uterus. The strong suction tears the baby apart, extracting the infant through the tube and into a jar. The abortionist must then "reassemble" the dead baby's parts to ensure that none were left inside the womb, which could cause an infection.

Dilation and Curettage (D&C)—Performed between 7-12 weeks of pregnancy. A sharp surgical instrument is used to invade the uterus and dismember the baby's tiny body.

Dilation and Evacuation (D&E)—Similar to D&C, except that forceps are used to twist and tear away the baby's body, which by now has developed solid bones. Bleeding is profuse. This method is so gruesome that many hospital staff and doctors refuse to perform it.

Salt Poisoning (Saline Injection)—This second-most common method is used after 16 weeks of pregnancy. The abortionist inserts a long needle through the woman's abdomen, penetrating the baby's amniotic sac. The child is forced to swallow the toxin, poisoning him/her to death. The baby's skin is also burned off. It takes about an hour for death to occur with this method. The mother then delivers a dead baby. Some children survive this procedure and are born alive. They do not live long.

Prostaglandin—Here, hormones are injected into the amniotic sac, inducing contractions that produce a violent labor. Usually the hormones are combined with other chemicals that help ensure the baby dies, though the risk is great that the baby will survive. There is a risk to the mother as well, including the possibility of cardiac arrest.[30]

Dilation and Extraction (D&X)—Using forceps, the baby's legs are pulled out, followed by the torso, arms, and shoulders. The baby's head typically remains inside the uterus. Then, with blunt-tipped surgical scissors, the baby's skull is pierced and a suction catheter is inserted, extracting the "skull contents." Fetal brains and organs are often used for experimentation.[31]

As you can see, notwithstanding the abortion industry's efforts to sanitize and minimize it, the horrific sin of abortion is neither painless nor easy. Destroying and removing an unwanted baby from a mother by another person is clearly an unnatural and immoral act. A woman must suppress every known maternal instinct in order to seek an abortion. And yet, this is how we kill our children in America, with the full blessing and endorsement of the US Supreme Court.

To the calloused conscience, the truth about abortion is anything but obvious. But to the biblically informed mind, however, the real reason abortion is so widely accepted and available is easily discerned. Satan's hatred of humanity and the self-centered depravity of the human heart are the fountainheads of this river of blood. Everything else (the media, politics, laws, health care, women's rights) are all just demonic smoke-and-mirror tactics intended to distract us and deflect our attention elsewhere.

Some may argue that the Bible never specifically says anything about abortion. The weakness of this reasoning is obvious. If we justify a practice solely on the grounds that the Bible never specifically forbids it, then we open up for ourselves a Pandora's box of wickedness. The Bible never speaks about pedophilia or crack cocaine either, but to conclude from this that they are not only permissible but morally justifiable is both illogical and absurd.

What the Bible does clearly affirm is illustrated by the following syllogism:

A. Murdering a person is wrong.

See Genesis 9:6; Matthew 15:19; 19:18; Mark 10:19; Luke 18:20; John 8:44; Acts 3:14; Romans 1:28-29; 13:9.

The unborn is a person.

Unborn beings are affected by sin and can experience joy and external stimulation, and in the case of John the Baptist, even be filled with the Holy Spirit. They are created by God, known by Him, and considered children from the moment of conception (Psalm 51:5; Isaiah 49:1; Jeremiah 1:5; Matthew 1:20-21). At times they are even referred to as "baby" (Luke 1:41, 44). The law God gave Moses declared the unborn as human and worthy of full protection and rights due an adult person. To injure a mother or her unborn child carried a penalty, including death (Exodus 21:22-23).

B. Therefore, murdering the unborn is morally wrong.

No one, Christian or otherwise, denies the pain and suffering experienced by a woman who is raped. No person deserves such indignity. And the aftershocks of such an experience often lead to severe psychological and emotional distress and problems. Further, it is understandable that an unplanned pregnancy may produce an initial feeling of shock, despondency, and even regret in some women. But as inconvenient and life-altering as that experience may be, the fact remains that it does not morally empower a women to murder the child inside her. Once a life is conceived in the womb, intentionally or otherwise, everything changes. The pregnancy may not be welcome, but the baby will be by someone.

For any woman reading this who has had an abortion, or any

man who has supported such a decision, guilt, shame, and confusion are not your only options. Thankfully, there is hope, restoration, and permanent forgiveness through Jesus Christ. God understands the ongoing psychological impact and emotional fallout that result from having made a decision in favor of abortion. But no matter how heavy your guilt, if you confess your sin to Him, through Christ you can not only receive and experience forgiveness, but be freed from the lingering guilt that accompanies such sin.

You may also need pastoral counseling going forward. Repentance brings healing and restoration, while denial and defiance bring negative spiritual consequences.

A Nation in Crisis

We live in a country where, at political conventions, those who speak of their decision to kill their children because "it wasn't time to have a family" are met with loud cheers from the audience.[32] Popular Hollywood actresses campaign for abortion rights. In 2015, the #shoutyourabortion twitter campaign went viral. These advocates are on a mission to convince America that abortion is "normal," and that there is no "debate" about it. The time for shame and silence is over. They want women everywhere to "shout" their abortion to the world.

Really? *Shout* your abortion? Could there be any greater expression of unrepentant sin than this? Do we seriously want a nation where potentially half of all women publicly brag about murdering their babies? Could this be any more of an incarnation of Isaiah 5:20 and Romans 1:29-32? Do we want to boast about the one million abortions that take place in the United States each year? Should more than 2700 women a day "shout" their abortion to the world? And yet we live in an age that "brags about shameful things"

(Philippians 3:19 NLT). This is the very personification of the blasphemous spirit so prevalent in the last days' generation (Revelation 16:9-11).

According to the Guttmacher Institute, in this country alone, about 53 million have been murdered in the womb from 1973-2011.[33] About 56 million abortions are performed worldwide each year.

Abortion is not mandated by our government, but has been declared a right granted by the government, with doctors and abortion clinics given "license to kill" status. In this sense, it is state-sponsored genocide way beyond what men like Hitler, Himmler, and Heydrich could have ever imagined.

The country's largest abortion provider, Planned Parenthood, currently receives a half a billion dollars in government funding each year. Though it maintains that abortions are only a fraction of the "medical care" provided by their clinics,[34] the fact that American tax dollars are used to fund this mass murder makes us complicit.

But past the abortion clinics' waiting room door, smiling faces, comforting voice tones, clinical procedure rooms, and lab coats is a sinister deception. Suppressed and concealed is the fact that abortion is not the mere removal of tissue, but the murder of the innocent. It's just another cleverly disguised ploy, birthed in the heart of the one who was a murderer from the beginning. And according to Jesus, if you lie and murder like the devil, you prove yourself to be his child.[35] Born out of paganism, self-worship, and a twisted, feminist, goddess-like exaltation, abortion is the indelible stain soaked into the soil of every state in the Union.

This national sin is damning testimony to the fact that our country is in perilous decline, and further evidence leading to a guilty verdict from heaven's court. We are not advancing, my friend. Rather, we are racing in reverse at breakneck speed, reverting to an ancient decadence and paganism.

It should be against the law to murder your own child. Period.

Despite what politicians and presidents may promise, America will never be great as long as abortion is legal and is allowed. And what are the chances of this law being overturned? Honestly, it's almost like we are taunting God, *daring* Him to judge us.

A Final Word

Through sanctioning and sanitizing the killing of America's children, we appear to have resurrected the same barbaric Canaanite spirit before whom Israel bowed 3000 years ago. Only this time, it has taken the form of self-worship.

Killing children is still the devil's business. And business is good.

But like those believers martyred during the coming Tribulation, the blood of innocent children also cries out from heaven for justice, praying, "How long, O Lord, holy and true, will you refrain from judging and avenging our blood…?"[36] God tells these martyrs to wait "a little while longer," assuring them that justice will be rendered and that every murderer will be held accountable for their sin. The same holds true for those who take life from the unborn. Justice and vengeance belong to the Lord. One of the seven things God says He hates and that are an "abomination" to Him are "hands that shed innocent blood."[37]

In a morally upright nation, there would be no abortion clinics or hospitals performing such heinous crimes. But we do not live in a morally upright nation.

The United States of America has run the table of Romans 1 sins, making her ripe for divine judgment. And with abortion, the level of our country's transgressions has crested the top of the levee. The dam is about to break, and with it will one day come a tidal wave of apocalyptic judgment. The only alternative to this wrath is nationwide repentance.

So will we humble ourselves, or will we be humbled?

Which will it be?

And what kind of future remains for America in a world preparing itself for the fulfillment of biblical prophecy and the end times?

6

Gog, Magog, and 'Merica

Unless we repent as a nation and reverse course,
I think God is going to bring quick and
swift judgment on this nation.[1]

—Franklin Graham

While being interviewed on a national radio show not long ago, a listener called in to ask, "Jeff, where is America in Bible prophecy? What is our role during the end of days?"

Whether you're a seasoned student of Bible prophecy or just now dipping your toe in the prophetic pool, it's pretty safe to assume you've asked the same question. It's normal to wonder if the United States is mentioned anywhere in the book of Revelation, or in any of the Bible's end-times prophetic scenarios. It's a fair question, and one worth addressing. However, at the heart of this matter lies a bit of confusion. For if the chaos and characters depicted in the last book of the Bible are still yet future, it does indeed leave us scratching our heads as to what all this means for our country. Why is it that many say this nation is nowhere mentioned in Bible prophecy, while others claim they see clear biblical references to the United

States? Who's right? Is it possible America is a prominent end-times player, and like other countries, remains intact until the second coming of Jesus? Or is there evidence to suggest we will simply vanish from history's radar and play no significant role in the last days?

Before diving in to uncover the answer, it's worth addressing another question first—namely, Why is there such curiosity and interest concerning America in Bible prophecy?

I suspect there are several reasons so many people desire to know the answer to this question.

First, we simply want to know what happens to our country in the end times. After all, it's our home and we care about it, right? Second, because of our Christian-based beginnings, it's somewhat strange to think that such a force for Christianity wouldn't play a major role in the last days. Third, America is the world's last real superpower. As such, how could we not factor prominently in global end-times events? Why would a smaller country like Turkey upstage a mighty nation like ours? The late great prophecy expert Tim LaHaye wrote, "One of the hardest things for American prophecy students to accept is that the United States is not clearly mentioned in Bible prophecy, yet our nation is the only superpower in the world today."[2]

Fourth, as citizens of this country, we kinda think we're a big deal. I mean, this is America the Great we're talking about here! As countries go, we're like the world's most famous celebrity nation. Our impact and influence are felt the world over. So perhaps there is a certain sense of entitlement we feel regarding our role in the end of history.

Some of these reasons are certainly understandable, for as we examine God's prophetic plan for the nations, it's only natural to wonder: Hey, what about us? Where are we in all this?

I believe there's a common mistake people make when studying

Bible prophecy—namely, that we try to make sense of prophecy by reading the times in which we live instead of making sense of the times in which we live by studying Bible prophecy. The first approach force-fits prophecy into today's headlines, while the other views those headlines through the filter of a biblical understanding of prophecy. It's the classic "Which came first, the chicken or the egg?" And in this case, it's the *chicken*. Current world events are not the template through which we are to read and interpret Bible prophecy. Just because something noteworthy is going on in the world doesn't, of necessity, mean it is prophecy-related or it has any direct connection to the last days. It *may*, but to find prophecy in every headline is to commit the serious interpretive error of *eisegesis*, or reading our own outside meanings into the Scripture.

Rather, we are to read and study the Scriptures, and then carefully sift the headlines and world events through that biblical filter. That way, we avoid running off the rails into needless speculation.

In reality, Bible prophecy actually *determines* the outcome of certain future world events.[3] Because a sovereign God is driving history toward its appointed end, we can be confident that what we see happening around us can only make sense when we have first grounded ourselves in Scripture. Again, to do otherwise is to make a fatal interpretive error that leads to wrong conclusions, misreading the times, and speculative and sensational claims. Every event, happening, and so-called sign must be held up to the light of Scripture in order to establish an accurate understanding of the times in which we live. When we apply a prophetic foreshadowing or fulfillment to the current world climate, we must adhere closely to God's Word. This doesn't at all mean we can't speculate or postulate possible scenarios, but those scenarios must be reasonable and stay within the parameters of what is found in Scripture.

The Players

Another important perspective to keep in mind is that the Bible devotes a substantial amount of content to primarily one nation—Israel. As God's covenant people, the Jewish people are a central character of the Old Testament as well as a pivotal player in the last days' Tribulation period. We often forget this focus on the nation Israel because we live in the church age, a time during which national Israel is experiencing what Paul calls a "partial hardening."[4] God's dealings with Israel as a nation have been put on hold while He brings about the "fullness of the Gentiles" during the church age. But when the future seven-year period known as the Tribulation begins, God will once again turn His full attention back to His covenant people in order to fulfill promises He has made to them and to save "all Israel" (verse 26). Concurrently during this time, He will also be dealing retributive judgment upon the Gentile nations of the earth.

Another fact to note is that, geographically speaking, the Bible is written from an Israeli-centric perspective. This not only is relevant to the events of end-times prophecies, but also to birth and expansion of the gospel itself, both geographically and chronologically (Acts 1:8; 8:1; Romans 1:16-17). The gospel originated in Jerusalem, and spread concentrically outward from there.

That being said, for those who are convinced we are living in the last days, it is reasonable to ponder whether the Unites States of America appears in the cast of nations mentioned in Scripture's prophetic literature. Of course, the good news is that the Bible does specifically mention many nations by name who are involved in end-times events. Aside from, of course, Israel, I have listed a few of them here. These are some of the countries named in prophecies related to Revelation, including what most biblical scholars understand to be their modern-day correlation:

- Rosh (Russia)

- Magog (Central Asia, Islamic Southern Republics of the former Soviet Union)

- Meshech and Tubal (Turkey)

- Persia (Iran)

- Ethiopia/Cush (Sudan)

- Libya/Put (Libya)

- Gomer (Turkey)

- Beth-togarmah (Turkey)[5]

These nations are a part of what has been called "the Gog Coalition," an alliance of countries who come together to attack Israel at some future time (possibly near the beginning of the Tribulation period).

Proposed USA Sightings in Bible Prophecy

You'll notice that the United States is not found in the aforementioned list, nor is it remotely related to any of the nations that do appear. Further, virtually all prophecy experts agree that nowhere in Scripture is America *specifically* mentioned. Even so, many prophecy teachers believe our country is still a part of the last-days scenario. And many even claim to have actually identified the United States in Bible prophecy. However, not all agree on where America is identified, and in what capacity. So the question then becomes, Are there any general or specific prophecies concerning the end times that could *allude* to or *include* America?

Here then are six views explaining how some see America identified in Scripture's end-times narrative:

View 1—America Is Babylon the Great (Revelation 18)

Here, parallels are drawn between the nation described in Revelation 18 and the United States. Babylon is described as being full of immorality (verse 3), a world superpower (verse 3), proud (verse 7), a place of wealth and affluence (verses 12-13), selling its goods and gold to the world (verses 11-12), helps other nations become rich (verses 3,19), once a light to the nations (verse 23), but suddenly destroyed in an hour, with the whole world watching the "smoke of her burning" (verses 9-10), a reference some relate to the 9/11 attacks.

From a cursory reading of Revelation's text, it appears there are some similarities between America and this future Babylon. However, I believe there are several problems with this interpretation. First, the Babylon of Revelation is specifically said to be a city, not a nation (16:19; 17:18). Second, of some 300 times Babylon is mentioned in the Bible, it always refers to a literal city. Further, 11 percent of Revelation (44 out of 404 verses) mentions Babylon in some capacity. If America truly is Babylon, she would be much more than merely *mentioned* in Revelation's prophecy. Rather, she would be a major focal point of the book!

View 2—America Is the "Eagle's Wings" of Daniel 7

Daniel received a vision of four world empires, which were pictured as a lion with eagle's wings, a bear, a leopard, and a fourth beast with large iron teeth. Out of the fourth kingdom arises ten "horns," explained in verse 24 as ten kings, subsequently accompanied by a "little horn," an obvious reference to Antichrist. The lion, they say, represents England, and the eagle's wings, the USA. These eagle's wings are "plucked" from the lion, which is interpreted as America's proclamation of independence from the British Empire in 1776.

I do not see this as a plausible explanation. Instead, I agree with the majority of prophecy experts, who see the lion of Daniel 7 as referring to Nebuchadnezzar and ancient Babylon. This interpretation is supported by the immediate context of the passage as well as history itself.[6] The eagle's wings being plucked correspond either with Nebuchadnezzar's insanity, the removal of Babylon's swift and powerful empire, or both.[7]

View 3—America Is One of the "Seven Heads" of Revelation 13

Revelation 13 portrays seven kingdoms that likely refer to seven successive world empires throughout history that have been energized by satanic influence. But as part of Antichrist's future rule, the last of these kingdoms is supported by an alliance of ten nations (10 horns). The problem with saying that America is one of the seven heads (kingdoms) is that in Revelation 17:9-10, these world kingdoms are all but identified for us. God's angel describes them this way: "five have fallen" (past tense)—Egypt, Babylon, Assyria, Medo-Persia, Greece; "one *is*" (present tense in John's day)—Rome; and "the other has *not yet* come" (future)—Antichrist's kingdom comprised of a ten-nation federation. If this interpretation is accurate, the United States cannot be one of the seven heads of Antichrist's reign as explained in Revelation.

View 4—America as the "Great Eagle" of Revelation 12:13-14

At some point during the Tribulation (most likely the midpoint), Satan will attempt a final coup on heaven, but will summarily be defeated and thrown back down to earth by the archangel Michael. Seething with anger, the devil will turn his attention toward the Jewish people he has betrayed, beginning a brutal persecution of "great wrath" against them.[8] In response, the Jews will flee ("fly") to the wilderness for protection, aided by "the two wings of the great eagle" (12:14).

America has long used the eagle as her symbol, and because of this country's strong historical support of Israel, it is concluded that we will somehow come to her rescue during this persecution, perhaps through some sort of massive airlift operation ("wings").

However, without knowing what America's position or power will be during the outpourings of divine judgment in the Tribulation, it is difficult to reach this interpretation. More likely the phrase. "two wings of the great eagle" refers to God Himself, as this exact imagery is used elsewhere in Scripture to describe how Yahweh delivered Israel from another pursuing tyrant (Pharaoh).[9]

View 5—America as the "Tall and Smooth-Skinned People" of Isaiah 18

In this obscure prophecy, Israel is cautioned by God not to make an alliance with "a nation tall and smooth," whose "powerful" land "the rivers divide" and is characterized by "whirring [buzzing] wings." Because Americans are often portrayed worldwide as beautiful, and our country is powerful and divided by the great Mississippi River, and we have a strong air force (i.e., "whirring wings"), this admonition must be referring to America, right?

This view actually gained some traction during the nineteenth century, but serious prophecy experts don't put much stock in it today. First, the context of the passage clearly reveals that God is speaking about Ethiopia/Cush in verse 1 (modern-day Sudan). There are several rivers that divide the country, the greatest being the Nile, and the "whirring wings" likely refers to the insects so common and plentiful in the Nile Valley area. Further, the people in that region (called Nubians) were a smooth-skinned people in that they kept themselves shaved. And last, at the time of Isaiah's writing, Ethiopia was a powerful nation, even ruling over Egypt.[10]

View 6—America Is the *"Young Lions of Tarshish"* in Ezekiel 38:13

At a predetermined time (likely in the early months following the rapture and before Antichrist establishes his prominence), a Russian-led attempted invasion of Israel will occur, accompanied by a host of Muslim nations (see the countries and their modern-day identities previously listed in this chapter). Their goal will be to once and for all annihilate Israel, which is a stated goal of many Islamic countries today. However, when this happens, several other nations will question this military action, perhaps even to the point of officially protesting it. Among those countries listed are "Sheba, and Dedan, and the merchants of Tarshish, with all its villages." Sheba and Dedan are in modern-day Saudi Arabia.

Dr. Thomas Ice goes on to explain,

> Merchants of Tarshish refer to the Phoenician maritime and trading community located in Spain during the general time of King Solomon, 3,000 years ago. The merchants of Tarshish, during the last 500 years, developed into the modern mercantile nations of Western Europe like Spain, Holland, and Britain. Third, the phrase "with all its villages" or the variant rendering "with all its *young lions*," would be a reference to its trans-Atlantic colonies, which would include America. Thus, it is reasoned, because America is the most dominant of these Western nations, this must be a reference to America.[11]

Tracing this line of reasoning may seem like a stretch for some, and at the end of the day, it is difficult to be dogmatic as to this interpretation. Is it possible that these "young lions/villages" refer to future countries colonized by the former "merchants of Tarshish"?

Yes, it's *possible*. But certainly not conclusive beyond a reasonable doubt.

Knowing Is Better Than Guessing

So where does all this leave us? What can we say with confidence about this nebulous issue? If America isn't specifically mentioned in the Bible, is there *anything at all* we can know for sure regarding our role in the last days? What *does* the Bible say…if anything?

Without speculating too much, let's first establish what America *has* done. Since Israel's rebirth as a nation, in which the United States acted in a sort of midwife capacity, we have been her staunch ally. This is not to say there haven't been disagreements and tensions along the way since Israel was recognized as a state. But more than any other country on the planet, we have stood by the Jewish nation, supporting and blessing her. In that sense, we have been used by God to contribute towards Israel's protection and preservation. With the exception of Barack Obama, whose snubs of the Israeli prime minister became famous, America and her presidents have, for the most part, been a real friend to the tiny Jewish nation.

However, in spite of our historically rich relationship with Israel, there is no guarantee that strong support will continue. It is unknown which way the geopolitical winds will blow in the coming months and years. But with growing fears fueled by increasing acts of anti-Semitism in our world, many Jewish leaders are calling for their people to simply "come home." And the Jewish people are responding, returning to a land that, despite constant dangers from Palestinian terrorism, welcomes them and offers them a safe haven.[12] Hopefully our current presidential administration will defy the prevailing spirit of the United Nations and continue to stand with Israel and the Jewish people. However, there are no guarantees this will happen.

Second, the United States, because of her strong Christian roots and the spirit of the evangelical church, has pioneered the modern worldwide expansion of the gospel. Through missions, church planting, Bible translation efforts, and even Internet ministries, America's Christians have impacted the world for Jesus Christ more than any other nation—through giving, supporting, training, and going.

These two factors alone are proof that America has *already* played a major role in these last days. But beyond these truths regarding the past and present, is there anything about the future we can affirm as it relates to the United States and prophecy? I believe the answer is yes, although the news isn't good.

Dr. Thomas Ice comments,

> Passages like Haggai 2:6-7, Isaiah 66:18-20, and Zechariah 12:2-3 speak of all the nations involved in end-time events. These kinds of references clearly will *include* the United States in their fulfillment, but they do not teach us anything specifically about America in prophecy.[13]

Possible Reasons for Scripture's Silence

As we've learned, during the seven-year Tribulation, Gentile nations will be the recipients of God's seal, bowl, and trumpet judgments. These are the nations whose collective sin, rejection of God, and refusal to submit to Him have earned them a sentence of hell on earth.[14] They have raged against heaven for centuries, and they will be made to drink a cup of apocalyptic wrath. God has pleaded with them through creation, conscience, Christians, the church, and even Israel, yet they have refused to give Him the honor He rightfully deserves. Eventually the age of grace will come to a close, and there will come a day that brings darkness, destruction, and death. They disregarded His patience, scoffed at His gift of love, and mocked His mercy.[15] God will laugh at them, mocking their pride and answering them with divine fury.[16] Certainly what's left of America in that day will be included in this group of world nations.

But the eerie silence concerning the United States in the last days has led some to conclude that we will no longer be a dominant power in the world at that time. There are many theories for this view (and I emphasize they are only proposed scenarios, though some seem more plausible than others).

Scenario 1—The United States Will Collapse Financially

As of this writing, our country is in debt to the tune of twenty *trillion* dollars.[17] Don't even try to wrap your mind around that figure. It's virtually impossible. According to *Forbes* and the US Census Bureau, 49.2 percent of US households "received benefits from one or more government programs."[18] Add to this a declining workforce and an underreported unemployment rate, and this cannot add up to a bright future for the country. And simply printing more money, though it may serve as a relieving, temporary Band-Aid, only further devalues the dollar.[19] All this is setting us up for a massive economic collapse unless a radical economic upswing occurs. If such a collapse were to happen, it would have a critical, catastrophic ripple effect on the average household, not to mention the fact it would increase our dependence on other nations.

The economic black hole that results from such a collapse would lead the country into virtual bankruptcy. Perhaps unable to maintain a military and pay our ever-increasing debts, we would eventually (voluntarily or unwillingly) be absorbed into a newly formed European coalition of nations. Due to our lack of bargaining power, we wouldn't even command the ability to be represented by our own nation's name. Instead, we could end up becoming part of some other European country. In this scenario, America would bear very little resemblance to her former self.

Scenario 2—America Will Collapse Morally

We've already talked about the grievous moral condition of America. In this scenario, America would completely bottom out in her moral freefall following the return of Jesus for His Bride. We'll discuss this in more detail in chapter 8.

Scenario 3—America Is Disabled by a Russian Nuclear Strike

In what could prove to be preparation for the eventual Gog and Magog invasion of Israel, Russia launches a preemptive strike, crippling any attempts the US could possibly make to come to Israel's defense.

Dr. David Reagan speculates,

> The Russian attack will probably come from submarines deployed off our East and West coasts. Each Russian sub carries more fire power than all the bombs dropped in World War II. Such a nuclear event would give us only seven minutes' warning, not even enough time to launch a counterattack.
>
> With the US immobilized, the Russians will then attack Israel in what is known as the War of God and Magog. But according to Ezekiel, their armies will be supernaturally wiped out by God on the hills of Israel (Ezekiel 39:14). The greatest power vacuum in the history of mankind will be created almost overnight. And the world will be gripped by panic.
>
> Into that vacuum will step a dynamic, charismatic European political personality who will be energized by Satan. He will begin to rally the world to his support through

his brilliant proposals for world peace. The planet will
be mesmerized by him (Revelation 13:8).[20]

Our current generation is far removed from the height of the
Cold War and the accompanying threat cloud under which we lived
in the 1950s and 1960s. It seems strange to imagine public schools
in America today practicing "duck and cover" atomic bomb drills.
Because of this, we have trouble imagining a nuclear strike could
really happen. But in a world where instability is normal and everything good is being eroded and replaced by evil, anything is possible.

Scenario 4—America Suffers a Cataclysmic, Crippling Terror Attack

No one reading these words has to be reminded how 9/11 is a
historical hinge on which the twenty-first century swings. Its effect
on our society and impact on our daily life indelibly marked us as
a nation. Some 3000 Americans were killed that morning, sending
America's commerce to a grinding halt and injecting a spirit of terror into our national bloodstream.

An attack of that stature could likely happen again—or, we
could face a preplanned, coordinated series of catastrophic attacks.
There is one thing we can be sure of: Radical Islamists are *not* going
away. On the contrary, their bloodthirsty brand is growing. It's not
a matter of *if*, but rather *when* we suffer another terror attack. Their
fanatical jihad is not fueled by a fleeting feeling of protest or dis-
content, but rather empowered by an unholy hatred whose origins
stem from the heart of Lucifer himself. Those who subscribe to
these terror-laced teachings are infected with an enmity that traces
back to even before the founding of Islam itself. Satan hates Jews,
Christians, and indeed, all humanity. His compulsion is to murder.[21]
And apparently part of his strategy has been to brainwash some of

mankind to adopt a religious ideology that involves becoming ruthless barbarians.

The reality is that there are currently more than 900 active FBI investigations into jihadist/ISIS-related activity that include all 50 of our states.[22] It is clear that something is brewing, and that this religious savagery is nailing its tent pegs into American soil. In addition, others claim there is irrefutable evidence of some 35-plus homegrown terrorist training compounds within our country's borders.[23]

Could America's economy, transportation, commerce, and even daily life come to another screeching halt at the hands of radical Islam? Does that sound far-fetched? Too fantastical to believe? Or could it be that we have grossly underestimated our enemy's ability to unleash death and bedlam into America's streets and homes?

It is unclear which, if any, of these four scenarios best describes what this country will look like in the very last days. And though these are speculative, they are *not* inconceivable.

Any one of these scenarios, or others not yet imagined, could easily become the catalyst that cripples the United States, causing us to be absorbed or assimilated into a European-based revival of the Roman Empire.

Focusing on What We Know

We may not definitively know all the answers about America's full role in prophecy this side of heaven, but you can bet the people who are alive during the Tribulation will have a pretty good idea. And even though not specifically mentioned in Scripture, I believe our country has already impacted these last days, and may still play some future role in the end times, albeit minor. Even so, we must not become too preoccupied with the things we don't know about prophecy, while ignoring the things God *has* made clear to us.

Bible prophecy was written primarily for the church, not the country. Jesus's main apocalyptic concern was not with first-century Roman culture, but rather with His beloved bride. Revelation wasn't written as an op-ed rant in the *Roman Times* newspaper. It was, and is, a holy document—penned to spur toward purity those who have been called out to follow the Christ.

So what will become of America if Jesus's bride fails to wake up?

From Isaiah 40 we learn that heaven's unrivalled God disposes of Gentile nations as He pleases, largely due to their arrogance and dismissal of Him. Like dust, He blows on them and they are no more. It remains to be seen whether America will survive to the end times. And if she does remain, her strength and condition are, as of yet, unknown. That truth alone should rouse us from our sleep, calling us to prayer and action for our beloved nation.

7

THE COMING PERSECUTION

What the situation will be like before the Lord returns,
Namely, Christ will be despised, and the preachers
of the Gospel will be regarded as fools.[1]

—MARTIN LUTHER

Mosul, Northern Iraq: A Christian refugee family is torn apart when their four daughters are forcibly kidnapped by ISIS terrorists. While their children are being held, mom and dad hold their breath, silently praying they would be rescued or returned safely back home. But they did not have to wait long for their answer. Within days, there was a knock at their door. Opening it, they found several large black plastic bags. Inside the bags, to their horror, they discovered the dismembered remains of their beloved daughters. Bags filled with body parts. Adding more gore to their grief, included with the bags was a videotape that showed their little girls being brutally raped, tortured, and murdered.

Abominable stories like this are not uncommon in many parts of our world, as Christian persecution is on the rise. In fact, CNN reported that 2015 "was the most violent for Christians in modern history, rising to 'a level akin to ethnic cleansing.'" Citing a new report by Open Doors USA, a watchdog group that advocates for Christians, CNN said the group's research found that "more than 7,100 Christians were killed in 2015 for 'faith-related reasons,' up 3,000 from the previous year."[2]

Some organizations claim that number is grossly inadequate, and that actually tens of thousands more Christians die for their faith each year, many of whose deaths go unreported or simply ignored.

In Syria, Assyrian believers are forced to kneel, after which they are shot in the back of the head, all because they refuse to convert to Islam.

In Egypt, a 17-year old boy was beaten to death by his classmates for wearing a cross around his neck.

In Nigeria, a bomb attack destroyed a house of worship.

In China, a pastor's wife was sentenced to a labor camp for using religious curriculum in a kindergarten.

In Laos, Christians were fined for simply being Christians. They were also pressured to sacrifice animals to village spirits, and by doing so, to renounce their faith.

In Iran, a pastor received a death sentence for leaving Islam. After he was given three chances to renounce Christ, he was thrown in prison indefinitely.

In a village south of Cairo, a Muslim Imam issued an order to kill all Christians.

In the Sudan, two pastors were arrested without cause and held for eight months.

In Kenya, an Al-Qaeda affiliate based in Somalia, Al-Shabaab, massacred 147 Christians at a local university.

In Nigeria, the Boko Haram terrorist group killed more Christians in 2015 than any other terrorist group.

In Saudi Arabia and Egypt, there are blasphemy and apostasy laws used to persecute religious minorities, many of whom are Christians.

All across the Middle East, Africa, and Asia, Christians are being persecuted and killed for their faith. They are being beaten, shot, hacked to death, beheaded, dismembered of body parts, doused with gasoline and set on fire, drowned, tortured, raped, kidnapped, and kept as sex slaves. They are imprisoned, crucified, dropped in vats of nitric acid, and blown up by suicide bombers or with explosives tied to their own necks and detonated.

To that list we may also add death threats, assassination attempts, economic suppression, extortion, prohibition from enrolling in institutions of higher education, kidnapping, and being forced to live in substandard housing. Less violent but psychologically devastating forms of persecution include slander, mockery, insults, exclusion from community social events, ridicule, harassment, threat of lawsuits, loss of jobs, and the seizure of property.[3]

Apart from this, Christians are also threatened, discriminated against, and unjustly accused and driven from their homes to become refugees.

It is estimated that worldwide, some 100 million Christians each year are targeted because of their faith. "There are over 65 countries where Christians are persecuted."[4] Every day, our brothers and sisters are suffering, bleeding, and dying for their allegiance to Jesus Christ.

Currently, the top ten countries for Christian persecution are:

1. North Korea

2. Somalia

3. Iraq

   4. Syria

   5. Afghanistan

   6. Sudan

   7. Iran

   8. Pakistan

   9. Eritrea

   10. Nigeria[5]

Nine of these ten countries have 50 percent or greater Muslim populations. In fact, Muslims now account for the greatest source of Christian persecution. In some of these countries, the Christian population is less than 1 percent.

However, this list of ten countries was recently expanded to include another nation where experts consider persecution to be on the rise. That country?

The United States of America.[6]

Persecution is real. And it's coming.

Not overnight, but eventually this migration of hatred will reach our shores. But how? And when?

The persecution of Jesus's disciples dates back to Acts 7 with the martyrdom of Stephen. In fact, among Stephen's last words was this scathing rebuke of unbelieving Jews: "Which one of the prophets did your fathers not persecute? They killed those who had previously announced the coming of the Righteous One, whose betrayers and murderers you have now become" (verse 52).

Indeed, there is a centuries-old pre-Christian history of persecution dating all the way back to the first family, when Cain killed Abel because of his brother's righteous sacrifice. This history continued in ancient Israel, with the likes of wicked Queen Jezebel, who killed the prophets of the Lord.[7] Jeremiah suffered under governmental persecution.[8] Daniel, Shadrach, Meshach, and Abednego were sentenced to death by pagan regimes.[9] The Jews were oppressed under King Ahasuerus during Esther's time.[10]

The author of the book of Hebrews tells us the righteous in the Old Testament were mocked and tortured, yet refused to compromise. They were scourged, stoned, sawn in two, put to death with the sword, wore sheepskins, goatskins, and were destitute, afflicted, and ill-treated. They wandered in caves and mountains and holes in the ground.[11]

Apparently, following Yahweh wasn't a very popular thing to do in Bible times. Nor is it popular in ours.

John the Baptist, Stephen, James the brother of John, and of course Jesus Himself could tell us what it's like to suffer at the hands of evil men. But persecution didn't end with them. The early Christians had their blood spilt at the hands of Roman emperors and officials. Generally tolerant, Rome considered Christianity to be a sort of superstition, and mistrusted Christians partially due to their perceived secretive meetings and strange customs. Rome had a flair for creative brutality the first few hundred years following the death of Christ. During that era, Christians were crucified, roasted over beds of hot coals, skinned alive, and sewn into animal skins except for head, hands and feet, then eaten by wild dogs. They were starved to death, boiled alive, ground to death in stone mills, scourged, and placed inside a brazen bull and cooked alive. They were penetrated with nails, spears, swords, and arrows. They were branded, pounded with clubs, had their tongues cut off, breasts amputated, limbs and teeth pulled out, thrown into rivers, branded, and exiled to hard labor.

And throughout history, though persecution has ebbed and flowed from era to era, it has nevertheless continued. During the Reformation, papal authority ruled over kingdoms and communities, threatening death to any who disobeyed. When the Reformers broke with the corrupt Catholic Church, the onslaught of persecution was merciless, with untold numbers burned at the stake for "heresy." And yet out of this alleged heresy Protestantism was born and the church was made spiritually pure so that it realigned with Scripture. It's ironic that religious groups and ideologies are often responsible, then and now, for some of history's worst eras of persecution.

Much Ado About Nothing?

So what are we to make of the ancient and modern persecution of Jesus's followers? Even with record numbers being oppressed and killed because of their faith in Christ, how do we know it will continue? Are these aforementioned stories nothing more than sensationalist narrative that makes mountains of persecution out of molehills of mere *opposition*? No. It was real then, and it's just as real now.

One of the problems Western Christians have is that we are largely uninformed about what is happening to our spiritual family members across the world. Compared to them, the church in America is a cruise ship of comfort, convenience, and entertainment. We must be careful not to be ignorant of other people's struggles, suffering, and death for the sake of Jesus. And we must not be complacent or compromising in our own faith.

So does the Bible have anything to say about the ill treatment or killing of Christians? Are there any prophetic passages that help us to understand what's currently going on, and prepare us for what may someday happen here in our own nation?

Fortunately for us, the answer is yes.

Final Instructions

Jesus Christ, in what has become known as His most famous prophetic discourse, spent part of His last week on earth specifically addressing the end times. Previewing for His disciples what life would be like for those who believe in Him during the last days, Christ lets them know they will one day be delivered to "tribulation," hated, and even killed on account of His name (Matthew 24:9).[12] During the Tribulation period itself, a false religious system will arise, uniting much of the world in idolatrous worship. And like the counterfeit Catholic religion of the Middle Ages, this ecclesiastical entity will also persecute true believers. In fact, spilling the blood of Tribulation Christians will intoxicate this "mother of harlots," filling her with a sick sense of euphoria.[13]

But Jesus provides further details, giving us added insight into the nature of this future Christian mistreatment. On the last night of that final week, He returned to this subject of hatred and persecution. He first let His followers know that they would be hated simply because they were His followers. Then He went on to outline five fundamental reasons why the world will hate and persecute His authentic disciples.

1. They hate Jesus and the Father (John 7:7; 15:18-21). Jesus said, "The world…has hated Me before it hated you" (15:18). Because unbelievers are born in sin and ruled by a depraved sin nature, they naturally resist, reject, and even resent God. When they mistreat His children, that mistreatment is actually an expression of their hatred of Him.

2. They don't know God (John 15:21). Jesus said if they really knew the One who sent Him (i.e., had an

authentic relationship with Him) they wouldn't engage in this sort of hatred against those who follow Him.

3. They resent having their sin exposed (John 15:22-24). God's truth is like an MRI, exposing the depths of man's sinful heart, all the way to his secret motives.[14] To some, this gospel news is refreshing, giving hope, while to others, it is smells like death, and for good reason.[15] The sound of the gospel is the death knell to the sin nature, and they know it. In fact, the message of the cross in itself is offensive, as it confronts the god-self and sin residing in each of us. It tells us we are ruined, separated from God and in desperate need of a Savior.

Therefore, when the light of His truth, verbally shared or displayed through a lifestyle, exposes sin and guilt, the response is either repentance or repulsion.[16] But according to the God of heaven, this hate is unjustifiable (John 15:25).

4. They see themselves as more righteous than Christians (John 16:1-4). Employing a twisted understanding of good and evil, some will morally elevate themselves above biblical values, labelling Christian "love and truth" as "hate and bigotry" (see Isaiah 5:20).

5. They recognize that Christians are not a part of their world system (John 15:19; 17:14-15). As Christians, we can sometimes be so wrapped up in daily life that we forget that this world is not our home and that its values are not our own. It's sad and ironic that unbelievers are sometimes more discerning than Christians in this regard. People who live by the sin nature within and abide by the godless world system controlled by the god

of this world can intuitively sense when a Jesus-follower and His counterculture morals and truths are invading their space.[17]

The apostle John later wrote, "Do not be surprised, brethren, if the world hates you."[18] So it should not come as a surprise to us that a secular culture and those who live in it would oppose the advance of Jesus's gospel and kingdom. Both are a deadly threat to the self-monarch who reigns supremely in the throne room of their hearts.

The Lord has already told us how bloody this hatred will become during the Tribulation. But how bad will it get in the days leading up to that apocalyptic hour? Paul gave us a clue in his final letter to the young pastor Timothy. He prophesied that "in the last days difficult times will come" (2 Timothy 3:1). He then described, in great detail, what the world will be like in those last days.[19] People will become increasingly selfish and narcissistic. They will be shallow, arrogant, materialistic, sinister, and unloving. They will be increasingly immoral and ungodly. Those who are religious will put on a public form of godliness, but will deny its power with their lifestyles. They will oppose the truth of God while promoting a twisted version of Christianity.[20]

Paul then said, "All who desire to live godly in Christ Jesus will be persecuted…evil men and imposters will proceed from bad to worse" (2 Timothy 3:12-13).

You see, currently, most unbelievers don't care all that much whether or not you are a Christian. But what they can't tolerate is when you open your mouth about your faith, take a public stand for it, or call their culture out for its sin. That's when the fires of persecution are lit and stoked. We may think that the world and Satan were satisfied when they persuaded Jewish and Roman authorities to torture the Son of God, putting Him to death on a cross. But, no. The hatred did not die on that black Friday.

The world is not finished persecuting Jesus.[21]

Instead, the persecution continues to this day, even picking up speed in this final season of history. Jesus's actual physical body ascended to heaven prior to Pentecost, but we, the church, are now His body on this earth. Unable to personally attack Jesus, Satan goes after His physical representatives. To touch us is to touch Him, and Satan knows it.[22]

Think about this: Jesus Christ was the most loving man our planet has ever known. And yet the world could not wait to kill Him. You are not better than Jesus or more loving than He. And though we must demonstrate uncommon love to all people—regardless of their sin—we must also recognize that this love will eventually lead to a gospel confrontation. And for some, that's when things get ugly. If they persecuted Him, they will most assuredly persecute you.

So we can say that Jesus and Paul's prophetic words regarding persecution have a "near fulfillment" (from first century until the rapture) and a "far fulfillment" (during the Tribulation period). So if that's the case, what then does persecution really look like from a practical standpoint?

Pipelines of Persecution

No Christian desires persecution. And we should never develop a "persecution complex" mindset. Even so, this does not alter the reality of Christian opposition, nor does it change our responsibility to prepare for it.

Satan is a master schemer, with a network, seen and unseen, of sinister avenues by which to deliver doses of persecution to the body of Christ. Here are some of his more obvious vehicles:

1. *Government*—The United States has historically been a haven for Christians, thanks in part to both our country's biblical beginnings and its fundamental commitment to the preservation of a free society. But as we've seen, governments are only as good as their leaders. As such, depending on the leadership, a given administration can change policy and law within a very short time period. While Christians have traditionally enjoyed much freedom when it comes to practicing our faith, that freedom has been challenged in recent years.

For example, the Obama administration led the way in legislating immorality, facilitating fatal fissures in the dam that held back evil and indecency for more than 200 years. Partnering with the Supreme Court, President Obama's administration mandated edicts and laws that not only declared sodomy to be as morally upright as biblical marriage, but also legally required all employers to provide expanded health benefits that include contraceptives that Christians believe to be abortion-causing.

And when any government makes it difficult for believers to stay in business because they refuse to violate their conscience and the Word of God, that becomes a not-so-subtle form of persecution. For instance, a Christian baker refused to make a cake for a wedding between two homosexuals because doing so would violate her conscience. She was sued and lost her business. Will America's churches one day be forced, under threat of having their tax-exempt status removed, to comply with the same hiring regulations as secular companies do? Will churches be required to comply with non-discrimination laws and be pressured to hire individuals who clearly violate the church's long-held beliefs? Will the refusal to perform gay marriages trigger fines or potential jail time for ministers? Just how much will secular government infringe upon our religious freedom and justify it all in the name of "tolerance" and "equality"?

Of course, compared to what will eventually come, our present government clearly is the "JV team." During the Great Tribulation under Antichrist's regime, the False Prophet will force all earth-dwellers (including those who have come to faith in Christ) to worship the Beast under threat of economic ruin and execution (Revelation 13:15-17). I believe we are living in the prologue of that prophetic book, and I anticipate an escalation of persecution leading up to that dark chapter in history. From John's apocalyptic vision, we know that humanity will one day develop a worldwide bitterness and unrepentant hatred for God and His Son, Jesus Christ.[23] The more God's wrath descends on the earth via the seal, bowl, and trumpet judgments, the more mankind will blaspheme and curse God, as those who hate God also hate His children. And the blood of Christians will flow.

In some ways history is coming full circle, with postmodern times resembling the ancient Roman era. As the spirit of the age grows more hostile toward believers, expect the winds of persecution to pick up.

2. *Culture/Social Media*—You could say that hateful attacks on Christians via social media could be categorized as "persecution lite." And to a large extent, you would be correct. What people say in social media posts does very little actual harm to believers. "Sticks and stones," right? But oddly enough, in the bizarre world in which we live, social media is the new "sidewalk marketplace" of American life. It's where people traffic ideas and connect with an ever-increasing network of contacts and friends. Currently, the number of Twitter users worldwide equals the entire population of the United States. Close to two billion people are regular users of Facebook.[24] And far from simply being places to post pictures of food and baby births, these social media outlets (including Instagram,

the blogosphere, Google, Pinterest, LinkedIn, Snapchat, and You-Tube) have become powerful outlets for marketing ideas, peddling philosophies, and accumulating followers.

In Jesus's day, a would-be teacher would strap on his sandals, locate a public venue, and start philosophizing in the hope of attracting a few disciples. Today, WordPress and BlogSpot have replaced the dusty setting of the ancient world. From the comfort of the kitchen table, a "mommy blogger" can post a few pictures about the farmhouse she's restoring, all the while composing posts about life, the mess in the laundry room, raising kids, and the struggles of marriage. The end result can be thousands of loyal, dedicated followers.

Of course, depending on the content, social media can be a very positive thing as well. But writing off social media as fluff can prove to be a naïve decision. The power and scope of what floats around in cyberspace often becomes the smoking gun leading to the death of one's reputation. A single Twitter post deemed homophobic or racist doesn't only attract vicious, personal online attacks and death threats. It can also lead to losing your job and being branded with a scarlet letter in the community. Employers routinely check social media accounts of potential employees to see if there are any red flags with regard to hiring the person. These days, scrolling through a Facebook feed can reveal more truth about a person's real character than five letters of recommendation.

So if a culture's values are predominantly un-Christian, it stands to reason that a majority of those on social media will respond with hatred and disgust at Jesus followers who infiltrate their world with biblical truth, especially if it directly challenges or threatens their deeply held beliefs. Should you doubt this, write a blog or a Facebook post against gay marriage or a woman's right to have an abortion. Share it and check the response you get. Post a blog about God creating the earth in six literal days and see what blowback comments come your way. Publicly declare the Bible is 100 percent historically, scientifically, and textually accurate, and then brace yourself for the counterattack. See what level of hostility fills your feed.

Obviously, there is a lot of good that takes place on social media. The medium itself is not the villain. But because social media is the new "preaching on the street corner," just be prepared for a few rotten tomatoes to be hurled your way. Or dead cats. As Christ's earthly repesentatives, we must always avoid being rude, abrasive, or unnecessarily offensive. In other words, we don't pick a fight just to pick a fight. That's begging for abuse. But just be aware that "being Christian" online could cost you friends and maybe even a promotion. And while obviously not as severe as other forms of persecution, it can lead to verbal attacks, severed relationships, and character assassinations. It's not beheading, but it is a beginning method of persecution. And for that reason it cannot simply be written off as nothing.

3. *Co-Workers, Classmates, Friends*—Sometimes Christians find themselves in situations where they feel compelled both by conscience and commitment to Christ to speak up for the truth. This is not always the case, as sometimes silence is the path of wisdom.[25] We are called to speak out against evil and to defend the faith, but that does not require us to constantly take on every moral or theological error we encounter. It would be impossible and futile to do so. Patience and prudence guide us in these instances.

Even Jesus Himself, in the midst of His own persecution, chose at times to remain silent.[26] However, at other times we are moved by the Holy Spirit to open our mouths to lovingly and clearly declare from Scripture the mind of God on a matter. And if we do, we must be prepared for the likelihood of retaliation. Doing this can cause tension in the workplace, classroom, and even among a friend group. For any time you "break with the pack" concerning a generally accepted belief, position, or value, the crowd may indeed suddenly turn on you, baring their fangs. And the wounds of a friend cut deep. This is the price of being a believer in a "crooked and perverse generation,"[27] and you must be willing to accept it.

4. *Family*—Sad as it may sound, our own flesh and blood can also be a source of persecution. In some religious traditions, those who convert to Christianity are not only disowned and disinherited, but are also considered as dead, and are sometimes even given a public mock funeral procession. Jesus forewarned His disciples that confessing Him as Lord would bring tension between family members, straining relationships.[28] In some cases, a separation occurs.

Some who are reading this know what I am talking about. And though it is not the believer who initiates this divisive spirit, a peaceful resolution is often not possible without some change of heart on the unbelievers' part. Unfortunately, until such a time, those estranged relatives must be loved from a distance. Jesus also spoke of a coming hour in history when parents, siblings, and children would turn believing family members over to the authorities to be put to death.[29]

Jesus said that.

5. *Radical Islam*—As previously stated, the majority of Christian persecution in the world today comes from the Muslim world. We in the West have trouble understanding how any civilized religion could dictate the torture, mutilation, domination, and death of all who fall under the category of *infidel*. But here is a concept we can and must comprehend: Muslims comprise the fastest-growing religious group in the world today.[30] At Islam's current growth rate, it is set to unseat Christianity as the #1 religion in the world by the end of this century.

Though the majority of Muslims are concentrated in the Middle East-Asia-Pacific realm, they are not content to remain there. Like Christianity, theirs is a religion dedicated to expansion, though employing radically different methods along the way. When conquering and destroying a nation isn't an option, Muslims simply immigrate…and wait. It is predicted that Islam will comprise 10 percent of all Europeans with a few decades.[31] Further, on average, Muslims have more children than those of other faiths, effectively breeding themselves as a means of fulfilling their mission.

Like people of other faiths, Muslims can be nominal and relatively harmless. They can also be radical and dangerous. The majority of Muslims here in the West are peaceful. However, *un*like Hindus, Buddhists, Mormons, and even those who practice the occult, radical Muslims are hell-bent on murdering us, destroying our society, and replacing our legal system with Sharia law.

That said, it only takes a small percentage of these fanatical Islamists to wreak havoc in a country. Their target is anyone who doesn't practice Islam, with a special cocktail of hatred and death mixed for Jewish people and Christians. In America, we have yet to see the long-term impact of Muslims permeating communities with mosques, burka-clad women, and the proposal in some cities to allow the practice of Sharia law. We have also not seen the fruition of potential Muslim attacks on Christians here, though given the encroachment of terrorist activity and Islamic ideology in the West, I believe this to be inevitable.

Radical Muslims do not always discern between those who are Christian and those who are simply part of a Christianized country. Their hatred is indiscriminate—in their eyes, America is the Great Satan, and therefore must be made to submit to their god, Allah. We've already witnessed mass shootings by Muslims in this country—murders of our military personnel and random, unpredictable attacks on individuals—under the battle cry of "Allahu Akbar!"[32] All through his presidency, Barack Obama consistently downplayed any terrorist attack's link to Islam, even though the evidence to the contrary was obvious and undeniable. I believe we will see a day in this nation when Christians and those who support them will become the primary targets of Muslim-borne persecution.

6. *The Church*—As unthinkable as it may sound, the organized church also plays a role in the unfolding drama of persecution. And why should this be so surprising? After all, the dominant religious force for hundreds of years, the Catholic Church, was responsible for killing untold numbers of true believers and persecuting those whose heart cry became "Sola Scriptura, Sola Fide, Sola Gratia" (by Scripture alone, by faith alone, by grace alone). Religion without the Holy Spirit has always been a dangerous entity, and an enemy of the cross. Bear in mind, the most prominent Jewish religious leaders were the ones who incited mobs, arranged for Jesus to be arrested and tried, and who lobbied for His death by crucifixion.

Religion apart from the new birth is merely a sanitized, ecclesiastical tool in the devil's hands. All across America, there are churches where the Spirit's absence is apparent, despite their activity. These churches have abandoned orthodox doctrine and the preaching of God's infallible Word, replacing it with either dead liturgy, self-help seminars, or entertainment. In many cases, they have become altogether apostate.[33] It is not just that they have "left [their] first love," but rather, Jesus has actually left *them*![34] I don't anticipate church congregations who embrace immorality and who are theologically apostate to physically harm believers in the last days. But as the divide between truth and false doctrine widens, I do see them contributing to ridiculing and marginalizing Jesus's bride.

The Stages of Persecution

The persecution of a people group is not something that happens overnight. Rather, much like a physical birth, it is conceived, then nurtured, and grown until it reaches its final mature form. So what are the gradient stages of persecution? What do they look like?

Here are six levels of persecution we see in the world today. Some of these overlap or share similar characteristics. At times, they can even skip over one another, quickly leapfrogging to a more intense level. See if any of these stages rings a bell:

1. *Negative Sentiment*—This is a general feeling of disapproval. It's not hatred or intolerance, but merely views Bible-believing Christians in a less-than-positive light. The name-calling starts, while the stereotype press goes into full production. It may include some scoffing and mocking, which Peter prophesied will increase in the last days (2 Peter 3:3-4).

2. *Demonization*—Here begins the official campaign. The "blame game" begins. We have seen this in our country when politicians, gay rights activists, and ACLU lawyers have used Christians as scapegoats, even to the point of blaming them for Muslim-motivated terrorist attacks. The reasoning goes something like this: "If those fundamentalist, ultra right-wing Christians hadn't created such a homophobic 'anti-queer climate,' then Muslims like Omar Mateen would never have killed 49 people and injured 53 others at a gay nightclub in Orlando, Florida."

This actually happened. Instead of radical Islamic ideology being blamed for what happened in Orlando, the "Christian right" and "homophobic" Christians took the hit in social media and some news outlets. Even Muslims jumped on the anti-Christian bandwagon, claiming that this kind of bigotry against gays is similar to what *they* experience with Islamophobia.[35] Inevitably, someone then brings up the Catholic Church's past and rants about the Crusades and other more contemporary corruptions and hypocrisies by professed Christians. The end result? Christians and their Bibles are now the bad guys, not the man who pulled the trigger.

3. *Marginalization*—So now that we know Christians are bad and are an obstacle standing in the way of progress, freedom, and equal rights, it's time to begin the "cleansing." As we've seen, our country is no longer a "Christian nation," and the pressure on believers to "keep it to yourself" means no Jesus "PDA" (public displays of adoration). This is sort of a reversed version of "Don't ask. Don't tell." So get rid of that nativity at the courthouse, and remove the cross from the war memorial. Let's not say "Merry Christmas" in department stores (offensive to Jews, Muslims, and atheists). It's time to drive the Christian faith out of the public square and confine it to church buildings, where it belongs. Their unstated goal is that Christians would no longer have a voice in our country. In this way, Christianity is "socially criminalized."

4. *Discrimination*—Because Christians are bad for society, they are also bad for business. Christians (and I'm not referring here to church-attending "nice people," but rather fully devoted followers of Jesus Christ) may not move up the employment ladder as fast as others. They may not even be hired at all. Christian athletes are mocked for praying. Christian doctors and scientists are denied their justly deserved recognition, or ridiculed for deferring to the Bible over "science." Christian professors are passed over for tenure. And though outspoken Christians may achieve success in their field of profession, their "superstitious faith" becomes a black mark on their record. If you want to see how committed Christians are to their Lord, hit them in the paycheck and see if they hold fast to their integrity.

I personally know a brilliant doctor, scientist, and inventor who is also one of the most dedicated Christians you will ever meet. Unjustly passed over for the Nobel Peace Prize in medicine (partly due to his belief in creationism), he turned down a check for $80 million for the rights to his invention because it would violate his conscience before God. But though others vilified and ridiculed him, he survived and rose to even greater prominence in his field.

5. *Criminalization*—Here is when the gloves come off—when laws are passed that make it illegal for Christians to follow the Word and ways of God. Churches, businesses, and schools are forced to comply with laws that directly contradict their deeply held religious beliefs. If they refuse, they are treated like all other criminals. They are either sued or arrested. And the penalties and fines for such governmental defiance can lead to the complete shutdown of their business or ministry.

6. *Martyrdom*—Thankfully, Christians in America have not been subjected to the kind of regime oppression and mob behavior so prevalent in other countries. As the writer of Hebrews noted, "You have not yet resisted to the point of shedding blood in your striving against sin" (Hebrews 12:4). However, in a world culture that is becoming more pagan every year, expect to see continued physical abuse and murder of believers across the world.

Faith and Fallout from the Coming Persecution

So as hostility against true Christians and their beliefs continues to escalate in the last days, what can we expect to see here in America? What will be the effects of growing persecution on the body of Christ?

I believe the greatest benefit of persecution will be the purifying of the church. When the going gets tough, nominal and casual

Christians will fall away. Some may realize they have never truly been saved and so choose Christ. But it will be a "come to Jesus" moment for authentic Christians too as they renew their faith in Him. This will greatly strengthen the church.

Those who desire comfort and compromise will put their boat in the lazy river of culture and float downstream with the rest of the unsaved. They will gravitate toward theologically liberal churches, embrace mainstream immoral agendas, and redefine Christian values such as unity, diversity, and love. Seduced by an emotionally based Christianity, their faith will be revealed to be a forgery, undetectable to all but those who are solid in Scripture, and "because of practice have their senses trained to discern good and evil."[36]

I anticipate many large churches will shrink in numbers, and correspondingly, their budgets will diminish as well. Churches will reevaluate the millions spent on lavish facilities, superfluous programs, and expansion campuses. The great "revival" for which many are praying may not be so much evangelistic in nature, seeing millions come to faith in Christ. Instead, it may involve those already saved returning to a fervency in their faith and love for Christ. For at the heart of Christianity is a life commitment to God. I am reminded of John 6, where we read that Jesus was followed by thousands because of the "positive perks" they could obtain from Him— namely miracles and lots of free food.[37] But then Christ turned up the heat, explaining what it really means to be His disciple. Bottom line, He requires total allegiance. And by the end of the day, thousands had disappeared, having fallen away.

After that took place, Jesus turned to His 12 disciples and asked, "You do not want to go away also, do you?" (verse 67).

Peter gave what has since become a much-quoted response: "Lord, to whom shall we go? You have words of eternal life. We have

believed and have come to know that You are the Holy One of God"
(verses 68-69).

In that short confession, Peter revealed the heart of discipleship
and what it means to be a Christian. A true believer is one who has
run out of options for hope and heaven, and has concluded that
Jesus is his only chance. He is persuaded at the deepest level that the
Word which comes from God is the only source of real life-giving
truth.

When persecution hits, those who are convinced of such things
are revealed as authentic disciples. Of course, talking a strong faith
means little unless our lives back it up. At times, even the strongest
believer fails and falters under pressure. Peter sure did—he caved
in when a little slave girl identified him as a companion of Jesus.[38]
But the apostle bounced back, having been convinced of another
great truth about this Jesus: that He had risen from the dead. After
the coming of the Holy Spirit at Pentecost in Acts 2, Peter became
a stalwart leader and spokesman for the church. Tradition says he,
like His Lord, died on a cross, and yet he requested that he be crucified upside down because he was not worthy to die in the same
manner as Jesus.

Though our faith will be tested when persecution hits, the grace
of God and the power of the Holy Spirit will enable us to persevere
and finish strong.

Much like our first-century brothers and sisters, I believe we can
also anticipate a growing opposition to the truth, which will impact
us in several distinguishable ways:

Persecution will draw a distinguishable dividing line in culture.
It will become much clearer who the Christians and non-Christians
are. It will identify us as disciples, and put a target on our backs. It
will be difficult to be a closet Christian. I remember the first time

I set foot on a secular college campus. Having lived in a Christian "bubble" atmosphere for a few years, it became abundantly clear that I was "not in Kansas anymore." In the classroom, the dorms, and on campus, the contrast between committed Christians and everyone else was obvious.

Persecution will force churches to make hard decisions about what kind of disciples they want to produce—consumer-driven attenders or Christ-filled world-changers. Persecution will help us clarify our priorities, recalibrate our mission, and purge us of Sunday performance-driven services and needless ministries that are a waste of time. It will radically change the way we "do church." One of the lessons we will learn is that the church's power was never in slick Sunday morning performances and presentations, but rather in the Holy Spirit (1 Corinthians 2:4-5). Our clever packaging of the gospel had no inherent ability to draw people to Jesus. The gospel itself has been enough all along. But why wait to learn that lesson?

Persecution will serve as a wakeup call to individual Christians to search their souls and prepare for Jesus's imminent return.

Persecution will bond believers together like nothing else. It will foster a healthy spirit of interdependence among those in the body of Christ. We will experience a level of encouragement between one another previously not known. Opposition to God and His people will only weave our hearts and lives more closely together in a strong-as-steel connection. Instead of merely showing up at church and glad-handing people at the coffee bar, there will be warm embraces of fervent love and comfort knowing that, outside of your own family, church is the only real "safe space" there is for you. You will appreciate the faith and public stand brothers and sisters take for the cause of Christ.

Suddenly for some, the Sunday sermon will take on a whole new relevance. There will be sacrifices made for those believers who have lost income due to persecution. It will be a time to rally around the hurting and wounded. We'll become tighter, more supportive, and more accountable. The increased opposition we face will cause us to say to our Christian family, "I desperately need you. I am depending on you." The early church had this. Why don't we?

Persecution will cause us to lose some degree of influence and popularity in culture.

Persecution will give us a fresh perspective on eternity and the brevity of life (Roman 8:16-18; 2 Corinthians 4:17-18). It will help focus our eyes past the here and now to the "not yet."

Persecution will fill our hearts with compassion for the lost as we realize even more than ever how much they are in need of salvation.

Persecution will cause us to rejoice and feel blessed that we were "considered worthy to suffer shame for His name" (Acts 5:41; see also Matthew 5:10-12; 10:24; Philippians 1:29; 3:10).

Persecution will be used by God to strengthen those believers who suffer under it, for the Lord gives an unusual grace to His own as they endure the hour of trouble.

And finally, persecution will frustrate and infuriate Satan, as through it, our faithfulness will ultimately bring greater glory to God.

So What Now?

Persecution, in varying degrees and forms, is coming. If it doesn't, then Jesus and Paul were wrong. The question is not whether it's coming, but rather how we will respond to it when it does. Some will undoubtedly give in and compromise, and in the process, deny Jesus. Others will initially seek to downplay persecution, perhaps even redefining it as simply a "misunderstanding." Still others may "go rogue," becoming more "underground" in their faith for fear of their peers, like Nicodemus, who approached Jesus secretly at night.

A better response would be to continue by faith, lost in love with the Jesus who refused to deny *you* while on the cross. For we know that nothing can separate us from His love.

Not even persecution (Romans 8:35-39).

And no experience we endure while on this earth is remotely comparable to the glory that will be revealed to us one day in heaven.[39]

The erosion of religious liberty and opposition to the gospel in America cannot dim the light of God's truth, or effectively shut up His children. As Peter and the apostles boldly declared, "We cannot stop speaking about what we have seen and heard…We must obey God rather than men."[40]

Knowing these things, we must be careful to avoid developing a persecution complex, yet at the same time not deny the reality of what's happening right before our very eyes. Because we have lived in a Christianized nation, believers have enjoyed a relatively easy road these past 200-plus years. But with the moral implosion we're experiencing in our nation, those days are over. It's only going to get worse as the floodwaters rise. How quickly they rise and how rapid those waters flow is up to God. But while we have the freedom to express and adhere to our Christian values and faith, we should not take this right for granted. Instead, we should cherish it, be thankful for it, and most of all, use it to grow spiritually and spread the gospel.

In the second century AD, a man named Polycarp was the bishop of Smyrna. He is also believed to have been the last surviving person to actually know an apostle, having been a spiritual son of the apostle John. But persecution was a clear and present danger in his day. And it eventually found him. After a warrant for his arrest was issued by a Roman governor, a search party of soldiers was dispatched for the hunt. Soon, Polycarp's secret hiding place was revealed after some of his acquaintances were tortured for information as to his whereabouts. Finding him at a farmhouse, he immediately responded by offering the soldiers some food and drink. The 86-year-old's only request was an hour of prayer before they took him in. They agreed, and upon hearing his cries to heaven, his captors wondered why a good man like him would ever be arrested. For this, he was permitted yet another hour of prayer.

When Polycarp finally appeared before the governor, he was given the chance to deny Jesus Christ and have his life spared. The old bishop's response was remarkable, and one for the ages:

> Fourscore and six years have I served Him, and He has never done me injury; how then can I now blaspheme my King and Savior?

As the soldiers prepared to nail Polycarp to a stake to be burned, the aged disciple assured them that no nails would be necessary. He would voluntarily stand and take the fire for his faith in Christ. It is said that as the flames were lit, they simply refused to touch the elderly man. Finally, a Roman soldier took his sword and thrust it into the body of God's faithful servant.

It would be inappropriate to compare ourselves with those who, throughout history and currently in other parts of the world, are suffering terribly for the faith. Every man and woman who names the name of Christ must walk his own path of faith, and if need be, suffer for it. What we are responsible for is to be bold and uncompromising in the culture where God has sovereignly placed us at this time in history.

And to face whatever opposition may befall us—with faith and grace.

8

WHEN THE LEVEE BREAKS

…America will perish unless she repents.
We have insulted the Almighty;
we are ready for judgment. But we need mercy.[1]

—Dr. Adrian Rogers

In the early hours of August 29, 2005, Hurricane Katrina made landfall in the Gulf Coast region of the United States. With sustained winds of up to 145 miles per hour, the Category 4 storm also brought massive amounts of water from the Gulf, creating a powerful storm surge that eventually weakened and spilled over the city's key levees. Billions of gallons poured into New Orleans, flooding over 100,000 homes and businesses. In an instant, thousands became homeless and were forced to search for high ground. Up to 75 percent of New Orleans's metropolitan area was submerged under water, as the devastation caused by this natural disaster would etch itself into New Orleans's storied history.

But apart from the hurricane's storm-related aftermath, there was also additional devastation. Looters smashed shop windows, stealing electronics, clothing, jewelry, and guns. Some of the city's residents turned into armed criminals, even shooting at would-be rescuers. Murders and rapes were reported while thousands of the Big Easy's citizens sought relief and refuge on bridges and in the New Orleans Saints's Superdome.[2] It was a storm New Orleans will never forget.

A hurricane is bad enough. I've survived five in my lifetime. But when the levee breaks, along with the rising waters, fear, confusion, lawlessness, and hopelessness also flood the streets.

Upon subsequent investigation, it was discovered that New Orleans's existing levees had not been sufficiently constructed to withstand such a storm surge. Though since rebuilt and reinforced, experts predict even these new levees would still have difficulty holding back another Katrina.

Levees are simply man-made embankments constructed to keep rivers from overflowing their banks or ocean waves from encroaching into populated areas. They hold back floodwaters and protect communities from disaster, keeping water from going where it shouldn't. But in the event one or more of them breaks, the consequences are typically catastrophic.

Satanic Storm Surge

In his second letter to the Thessalonians, the apostle Paul prophesied about a time in history when our world will experience something far worse and more devastating than a Category 4 hurricane. He wrote of a dark chapter in the human story when a figure will emerge out of the sea of humanity and onto the global scene.[3] This man is called by many names—the little horn, the "man of lawlessness," the "son of destruction," the "beast," "the prince who is to come," etc.[4] But his best-known title is "antichrist."[5] The same John who penned Revelation had earlier forewarned us that "antichrist is coming" and that the spirit of Antichrist was "already at work."[6] John also revealed that we are in the "last hour" of history

(1 John 2:18). And if the hour was late in John's day, where do you think we are now?

If you have read or studied about the end times, then you are aware of the divine judgments God will pour out on earth and its inhabitants during the seven-year period known as the Tribulation. But what other characteristics will mark this season? John informs us in Revelation 9:20-21 that a series of major *sins* will also command humanity's attention and allegiance during Antichrist's ascension to power.

> The rest of mankind, who were not killed by these plagues, *did not repent* of the works of their hands, so as not to *worship demons*, and the idols of gold and of silver and of brass and of stone and of wood, which can neither see nor hear nor walk; and they *did not repent* of their *murders* nor of their *sorceries* nor of their *immorality* nor of their *thefts*.

Admittedly, these verses almost sound unbelievable, too *bad* to even be true. They remind us of Genesis 6:5, where Moses described earth's pre-Flood population: "Then the LORD saw that the wickedness of man was great on the earth, and that *every intent of the thoughts of his heart was only evil continually.*"

Seriously? Did God really mean for Moses to write that? Don't you find it nearly incredulous that all of humanity filled the majority of their days with a constant, relentless pursuit of evil and sin? And yet there it is, right there in the Bible. Devoid of God and their consciences numbed by habitual sin, multitudes soaked themselves in unceasing corruption. John's synopsis of Tribulation unbelievers mirrors that of Noah's generation. Both have no intention of repenting, even though the way of salvation is offered to them. Revelation's author chronicles this future time when godlessness will once again thoroughly saturate the minds and hearts of humankind. Among these universal sins John lists are:

Unrepentant Hearts—People will stubbornly refuse to submit to God, even though they clearly acknowledge His existence and know He is the source of the Tribulation judgments (Revelation 6:15-17). This further exposes the depths of depravity to which the human heart can plunge.

Demonic Worship—Unwilling to repent and come to the true God, they turn to demons. Perhaps they fall for the lie that these fallen angels can somehow rescue them from heaven's holy terror. In this same chapter 9, John sees a vision of earth's inhabitants being tormented by millions of demonic creatures for five straight months. Is it possible humankind will attempt to appease these evil entities by worshipping them? There is a dark irony here as people worship the very demons who directly administer their suffering. This is the ultimate spiritual bondage. But it is God's wrath they should be concerned about, not that of demons. Also tragic is that Jesus Christ's substitutionary atonement at the cross completely satisfied God's anger toward their sin.[7] And yet they will still turn away. Someone has defined hell as "truth seen too late," a fitting proverb for those God-rejecters who suffer through this period.

A third possibility is that the lure of the evil so inherent within the demonic host is actually *attractive* to the sin-soaked minds of the Tribulation depraved. Idols crafted of gold, silver, brass, stone, and wood here are likely demonic representations. Having just come out of an age of unprecedented scientific and technological advances, mankind will return to uncivilized, pagan religious practices.

Murders—As in the days of Noah, this future time will be marked by blood-soaked soil. The murder rate during this time will likely skyrocket worldwide. It will indeed be a "survival of the fittest." With a spirit of entitlement gone mad, "What's yours is mine" will become mankind's mantra. No one will be safe in that day.

Sorceries—This word, translated from the Greek term *pharmakon*, can refer to "poisons, charms, amulets, drugs, magic spells or any object that bring relief, elicit lust, or be otherwise enchanting."[8] It can also refer to witchcraft. As drug use was common in conjunction with witchcraft in the ancient world, it is possible the two are combined here. Regardless, many will no doubt seek to escape the hell on earth through a perpetual mind-numbing haze of narcotics. The flow of drugs and addiction to them will hit an all-time historic high.

Immoralities—Sexual promiscuity, perversion, and deviance are additional characteristics of this day. What we learned earlier in chapter 4 of this book will dramatically increase in the final days.

Thefts—Rampant thievery, armed robbery, and widespread looting will create a climate of chaos across the planet. It will be a time when mass numbers of people have no regard for the rule of law. We're even seeing some of that spirit in America today. Law and order will become a thing of the past, cast away by an expediency brought on by global economic collapse and widespread fear.

What a world.

But what could possibly trigger such a deluge of demonic activity worldwide? What could initiate this kind of global godlessness? In the same passage where Paul reveals this future Antichrist, he states that there is only one thing currently preventing the man of sin and pandemic madness from sweeping the planet.

The "Restrainer."

> You know what *restrains* him now, so that in his time he
> will be revealed. For the mystery of lawlessness is already
> at work; only *he who now restrains* will do so until he is
> taken out of the way (2 Thessalonians 2:6-7).

The Thessalonian Christians were a confused bunch. They wondered if, as some had claimed, the "day of the Lord" had arrived, and whether they were already living in the final days when Antichrist would be revealed.[9] Paul's answer to the Thessalonians' "Are we there yet?" is an unmistakable "No." His inspired reasoning here is that before these events can occur, something else must happen—namely, the removal of "he who now restrains." There have been various interpretations as to what, or who, Paul was referring to here. Some have suggested it's government that restrains the lawlessness and sin we will see in the final days. And though this is part of government's ordained role, I don't believe this is an accurate interpretation, as governments will not be removed prior to the Tribulation; instead, they clearly continue on into it.

Others have speculated that it is the archangel Michael who currently holds back evil and the powers that seek to unveil the man of sin. Though this is theoretically possible, there is no contextual evidence here or in other Scripture passages to corroborate this view. Still others have proposed the Jews or the gospel as the restrainer.

But consider this for a moment: Whatever this restrainer is, it (he) by necessity must be *supernatural* in nature. Only a supernatural power could hold back Satan's desire and ability to unleash his Antichrist. Only something divine could currently be stemming a global tide of sin seeking to flood the earth. This is one reason why I interpret "he who now restrains" to be referring to God's Holy Spirit. Only a divine power equal that of God Himself could, for thousands of years, hold back the rising floodwaters of man's sin. But I believe there is also grammatical, theological, and prophetical evidence to support this view as well.

In verse 6, Paul uses both the neuter pronoun (Greek, τὸ κατέχον = "*what* restrains him") as well as the masculine (Greek, ὁ κατέχων = "*he* who now restrains") to refer to the restrainer. We know elsewhere in the New Testament that this neuter pronoun is also used when describing the Holy Spirit.[10] Obviously, whatever or whoever is described by the neuter pronoun in verse 6 also applies to the masculine "he" in verse 7. In other words, they are the same person.

Further, contending with man's sin and calling him to repentance while delaying judgment is something the Holy Spirit did on a global scale in the days of Noah.[11] Back then, His "striving with" or "abiding with" mankind revealed something of His role in the world—demonstrating God's patience and presence while calling people to Himself before judgment arrives.[12]

Last, Paul is here prophesying about a time when this restrainer would be "taken out of the way." But when would that conceivably happen? What point in time could possibly be on Paul's mind here? When in the future will God again remove His Spirit's influence from mankind in preparation for another global judgment?

I believe that event to be what many call the rapture of the church.[13]

This prophetic happening will occur at the end of the church age. Paul wrote about it in detail in his first letter to the Thessalonians.[14] The rapture refers to a pivotal moment in time when Jesus Christ will physically descend from heaven, snatch away His bride from the earth, and take her to heaven to be with Him before He releases the awful judgments described in Revelation.

But wait. You may be wondering: How God could remove His Spirit if He is omnipresent, or everywhere at once? Good question.

First, though there is no place God's Spirit is not present, even in hell, He does not *reside*, exert influence, or make His presence known in every place.[15] Because He is sovereign, the Holy Spirit uses His convicting and restraining influence only where He desires and when it accomplishes His plan.[16] Though present throughout the Old Testament, the Spirit's ministry has not always included *indwelling* all believers. That unique role began at an event called Pentecost. It was there, in Acts 2, when the Spirit descended to indwell believers, filling and empowering them for life and service. It was at this moment the church *officially* began—the Spirit came into the world to deal with sin and gather the bride of Christ together by bringing them to salvation. Through his sovereign power and working through the church, the Holy Spirit has also prevented mankind from totally saturating the planet in sin.

In the future, following the rapture of the bride, that restraining influence will be "taken out of the way." The removal of the Spirit's residence during the Tribulation does not mean He will cease to be omnipresent or that He will no longer draw men to Christ. Individuals will be saved during that time, but will not officially be a part of that special group known as the bride of Christ, for she will already have been rescued to heaven prior to Revelation's judgments. In this sense, Tribulation believers will be more like pre-Pentecost believers.

Similarly, just as the Spirit played an integral role in the birth of the church, so He will do so again in her culmination on earth. Dr. Dwight Pentecost wrote,

> The Church age commenced with the advent of the Spirit at Pentecost, and will close with a reversal of Pentecost, the removal of the Spirit. This does not mean that He will no longer be operative in the world, but only that He will no longer be resident upon the earth.[17]

As God the Father releases people and nations to their sin, removing His influence through divine abandonment, so the Spirit will remove Himself at the rapture.

Therefore, Paul's prophetic chronology here is as follows:

1. The Restrainer is "taken out of the way" (Thessalonians 2:6-7)

2. The "lawless one" or man of sin is revealed (verse 8)

3. The "day of the Lord" arrives (verses 3,8-9)[18]

Therefore, with the rapture event, it is Jesus Christ and the Holy Spirit who become personally responsible for this justifiable, worldwide levee break. But how else will the rapture play a key role in the resulting sin explosion and demise of America?

Signs and Seasons

We know from Scripture that Jesus's snatching away of His bride could happen at any time.[19] This is what theologians call "imminency," or the *imminent* return of Christ. This doesn't mean it is *necessarily* soon, but rather that it is *inevitable* (which could mean soon). It will also occur instantaneously. Faster than the blink of an eye, and tens of millions of Christ followers will be transported and translated from this world to the next.[20] In the time it takes a breath to exit our lungs, we're gone. Out of here. One second we are on earth, and the next we are "caught up…to meet the Lord in the air."[21] From there, we go to be with Him in heaven. This has been the desire of Jesus's heart from eternity past.[22] Meanwhile, those left behind on earth will experience the awful wrath of God, a vengeance that has been stored up for centuries.

The rapture's agenda, as written by Paul, is clear, though it all happens in an instant.

> The Lord Himself will descend from heaven with a shout, with the voice of the archangel and with the trumpet of God, and the dead in Christ will rise first. Then we who are alive and remain will be caught up together with them in the clouds to meet the Lord in the air, and so we shall always be with the Lord (1 Thessalonians 4:16-17).

First, Jesus will personally descend from heaven, accompanied by a loud voice, presumably His own. Not a whisper, but an audible, authoritative *shout*. This shout could be similar to the one Lazarus heard when Jesus summoned him to "come forth" from the grave.[23] His voice will be followed by another, this one from the archangel, Michael. Some prophecy teachers believe this voice is an "Amen!" to Jesus's shout. In this view, Michael serves a role similar to the shout heard in the parable of the ten virgins, announcing, "Behold, the bridegroom! Come out to meet him."[24]

With this voice is also the "trumpet of God," a further summons for the worldwide bride to assemble.[25] The trumpet was used in ancient Israel as a means of calling God's people together.[26] Here a special, sacred trumpet will be used for that same purpose. The word Paul chose here in verse 15 to describe the coming of the Lord is *parousia*, meaning "presence or arrival." This trumpet blast will be loud, and it will be music to a true believer's ears, declaring to us all, "It's time! He's here!" It's the sound we've been longing for these past 2000 years.

I want to be ready when that trumpet sounds. Don't you?

Next, the dead in Christ will be raised first, their spirits having journeyed with Christ from heaven. It is here, in the clouds, where they will reunite with their long-decomposed remains, brought up from their graves and supernaturally transformed into new, heavenly bodies.[27] Following this, those believers who happen to be alive on earth at this appointed time will be "snatched up" into the clouds to meet the Lord, be transformed themselves, and reunited with those who preceded them in death. Then, finally all together, the bride will enjoy God's presence in heaven while those on earth endure Tribulation.

The Last Gentile

Think of it: Some person will be the last to believe in Christ just prior to the rapture. God has ordained a specific number who will believe during this time we call the church age. Or, as Paul put it, "until the fullness of the Gentiles has come in" (Romans 11:25; see also Acts 13:48; 15:14). This is part of the greater "mystery" that is the church.[28]

Logically and theologically, then, one person will be the final one to trust Jesus for salvation before the rapture takes place. But who? Will it be a dying grandparent, calling out to God on his nursing home deathbed? Will it be a young teenager, responding to an altar call at youth camp? Or perhaps an addict, casting away dependency on drugs to trust in Jesus for salvation, survival, and deliverance? Could it be a wayward spouse or a bankrupted businessman, gun in hand about to end his life due to the effects of sin and the hardships of life? Or maybe it will be a four-year-old boy who puts his faith in Christ following a bedtime Bible story read by his mom.

Who is God "waiting on"? Just how many are left to believe before that "fullness" has come? Whose faith in Jesus for salvation will trigger the trumpet of God? No one knows except Him. But we *do* know there will be a *last believer*.

And that will signal the time of our departure is at hand. And though anticipated and expected, it will nevertheless be unforeseen. No person, regardless of claims or supposed evidence, can predict the timing of the rapture. And any who attempt to do so only expose themselves to be false prophets.

I have often wondered whether, after that last person comes to faith, there will be a brief pause in heaven while the angels rejoice.[29] Or could such a pause signal a silence in heaven for a short time, giving its residents an opportunity to reflect on the end of the church age? Perhaps a moment for the redeemed in glory to contemplate the mind-boggling phenomenon that *is* Amazing Grace? Or will that final exercise of saving faith instantaneously dispatch Jesus, Michael, and the spirits of heavenly saints to the earth?

These details are not revealed to us in Scripture. However, what we can be sure of is that Jesus will make good on His promise to return, and that His bride, courted and called throughout the last 2000 years, will finally see the day of her "blessed hope."[30]

When the Bottom Drops Out

During His ministry, Christ referred to His followers as the "salt of the earth" and the "light of the world."[31] The salt common in the Dead Sea area of Jesus's day was primarily used as a preservative. Before modern refrigeration, salt was utilized to prevent bacteria from poisoning food. Without it, a person may unknowingly consume contaminated or spoiled food.

In a secondary sense, pure salt both enhances flavor and produces thirst. Christians indwelt by the Holy Spirit, like salt, are part of God's "preserving" of civilization. There is a "sanctifying influence" we bring to culture, not simply through fighting evil and speaking out against immorality and injustice, but also through the positive contribution we make to society. Primarily through bringing others to faith, Christians help "preserve" that which is good, honorable, and praiseworthy in culture. And by modeling wholesome, godly values regarding family and Christian character, we also help safeguard society from moral implosion.

But believers are also part of God's "thirst-producing" agents in the world today. A few years ago, I co-wrote a book with my friend, Bobby Conway, titled *The Fifth Gospel*. The theme of the book is reflected in a quote by Gypsy Smith, a nineteenth-century British evangelist who had said, "There are five gospels: Matthew, Mark, Luke, John, and the Christian. But most people never read the first four."

He was right. It's as true as the age-old maxim "You may be the only *Jesus* your friends ever see." By our lifestyles, we demonstrate to others the truth, reality, and attraction of Jesus Christ. And through our words, we bring the message of salvation and freedom from sin's slavery found only in Him. Our lives are walking advertisements that read, "Taste and see that the LORD is good."[32] So as salt creates a physical thirst, our words and lifestyles can create a thirst for God in the world.

But Jesus also appointed His disciples as the "light of the world." He had previously made this claim about Himself in John 8:12. But since the moment He ascended from the Mount of Olives sometime in the late spring of AD 30, His followers have served as His physical representatives in this role. Light *exposes* the darkness, as well as *penetrates* it. It also illumines and shows the way.

So imagine what will happen when both the salt and the light are removed from today's culture. Who will be left behind to preserve decency, morality, and goodness? Who will expose and penetrate the darkness? Even now, if every Christian were to give up on saving America, she would have little hope. If we conceded defeat in our war on injustice and immorality, our country would systematically self-destruct, collapsing under the weight of its own sin.

Evil is not effective without a host through which to spread its poison. It requires "the prince of the power of the air, of the spirit that is now working in the sons of disobedience" in order for it to flourish.[33] In other words, wickedness flows in and through the spirits of demons and people. It is also never passive, but is always moving to influence toward the darkness. God's Spirit, mightily working both outside of and through the church, is what is presently preserving our culture from a total saturation of sin. And this is not hyperbole. Without Christians present in post-rapture America, who do you think will make Americans thirsty for God and salvation?

Similarly, throughout other nations on earth, there will be no one to shine the light of truth and morality. Remove light and only darkness remains. Our government (or perhaps what's left of it) will struggle to function, as America and her leaders will be 100 percent made up of those who do not believe in God's Son or His Word. Not a single believer on American soil. Imagine that for a moment.

Even those left behind who are morally upright, including peaceful people of other religions and those with conscience, will be powerless to prevent chaos and wickedness from permeating the land. An entire citizenry will be swept away by a tsunami of sin and selfishness. With our country's soul now removed, she will become a zombie-like nation, wandering aimlessly toward her ultimate and inevitable demise.

So how else might this rapture event impact the world, and specifically, the United States?

In this miraculous moment, the complete departure of Christians is not the only thing that will change. Everything will be altered following that split-second departure—governments, states, communities, militaries, schools, churches, colleges, hospitals, universities, families, marriages, national infrastructures…*everything*. There won't be a single pocket of society that remains unaffected, as for all practical purposes, God will have "left the building."

What follows is political, economic, and moral chaos in this country.

No Christians means no Christian churches or organizations or ministries. Churches will become hollow houses of worship. No one will be present to actively fight sin anymore. No preachers left to preach the gospel. No missionaries to spread the gospel worldwide, as they will have vanished. Christian authors, speakers, singers, and evangelists will all have been rescued from the wrath to come. A colossal void of truth will be left behind. And unrestrained sin will begin swallowing up an entire society. All across the country the scenario will become one of confusion, chaos, and fear, resulting in rampant crime, robberies, and murders. A nationwide panic attack will grip the country.

Houses and businesses vacated by believers will be overrun, and their contents stolen, destroyed, or perhaps burned. Cars will have new owners, driven by opportunistic thieves who have just realized it's the end of the world.

Law enforcement personnel will struggle to contain the swelling crime wave. Presumably, martial law will be declared. Our military, itself also likely reeling from the hit suffered when soldiers and key leadership cannot be located, will be asked to help. The United Nations will hold an emergency session. In Washington, government legislators and political leaders will likely convene with their remaining colleagues in an emergency session to seek answers and to try to avert total anarchy. Our government has contingency plans for continuing to operate in the event of a nuclear attack or some massive disaster. But they have surely not factored in the devastating repercussions of a biblical rapture scenario.

Other religious leaders, pastors, and ecclesiastical dignitaries and millions of nominal church members all across America will share in their horror. It's possible that some of these people will drop to their knees, genuinely confessing Christ with saving faith after faking it for years. Others, still incredulous and in shock at what has taken place, will search for some rational explanation for the disappearance of so many persons. The scientific community, though perhaps not as hard-hit as other segments of society, may attempt to explain this event as having been caused by some sort of an atmospheric phenomenon. It's also possible they will appeal to a long-held theory regarding extraterrestrial life, speculating that some sort of global abduction has taken place. But it will be just another diversionary tactic by the enemy. More deceptive smoke and mirrors.

Philosophers will weigh in, as will a contingency of atheists, though in a very short time, their voice will be drowned out by the blaring reality of the seal judgments, during which time atheism will officially become extinct.[34]

Gurus and false prophets will arise, peddling their own web of lies, deceit, and alternative explanations in an attempt to capitalize on this global catastrophe.

America's military will be placed on high alert, as the post-rapture chaos will weaken our perceived strength in the world. Nations may rush to take advantage of the United States's sudden loss of military personnel and power, perhaps even launching some sort of missile strike on American soil. Or more likely, the coalition of nations we read about in chapter 6 may initiate their attack on Israel, now that her greatest ally, America, has perhaps been rendered impotent.

The days following the rapture may also serve as the impetus and opportunity radical Islam has hoped for. Obviously, 100 percent of this barbaric ideology's leaders, followers, and foot soldiers will still be here. Could it be they will use this as their chance to initiate a coordinated, coast-to-coast jihad in those countries into which they have immigrated and infiltrated? With training camps already functioning and covert terror cells firmly in place in key locations, could this be when they finally realize their stated goal of hoisting the flag of ISIS over the White House?

No doubt other countries and armed forces will also be placed on alert as international tensions and the level of volatility for world war reaches an unprecedented critical stage.

Because of the rapture, a significant portion of America's population will be gone, leaving huge voids in virtually every strata of society. Riots, looting, and murder will occur in every city on a massive scale, causing America's streets to run red. Those left behind will become emotionally unhinged. And no national political or religious leader will be able to bring stability and peace. The result will be that, because the rapture will remove the last vestiges of decency from our country, America's infrastructure will simply collapse. Our economy will tank, hitting rock bottom, as millions default on their mortgages. Many taxpayers will be gone. Tens of millions of consumers, along with their buying power, will be cut off from the marketplace, further crippling the economy. This will usher in the worst depression in human history.

With anarchy and chaos reigning, America will be paralyzed, and officially no longer a major player in world affairs.

Like a heavy blanket, darkness falls on the entire nation, covering the rest of the planet as well. However, in nations like ours, where the gospel enjoyed a strong presence, this sudden removal of salt and light will enact a devastating toll. It will be as if a global EMP (electromagnetic pulse) has hit, crippling the power grid and snuffing out the power, and thus the light. Think of it: For however long it takes for the first post-rapture person to repent and believe on Jesus, planet earth will be completely devoid of Christians. Not a single believer will exist in the entire world. From a truth-hating majority's perspective, those "hateful, homophobic, bigoted, racist, right-wing Christians" will finally be gone.

Yes, that's what America could look like without Christians and their Holy Spirit.

In the time it takes you to bat an eye, our country will be transformed from the Land of the Free to the Abode of the Abandoned. Before the sun rises again, she will go from being a global superpower to a drowning nation struggling to survive. And she will be joined in these deep waters by the international community, staggering from the domino effect of world economic collapse, chaos, and carnage.

Most people have no concept or mental construct for imagining our country with hardly a trace of God or His children. But take all the godly presence and influence away, and what you're left with is, well, *un*godliness.[35]

And though the rapture will start the final clock that ticks down toward the day of Satan's doom, this chief fallen angel nevertheless will regard the event as a fantasy come true. Now that the body of Christ and the Holy Spirit's restraining influence are gone, it becomes *his time*. Aware that time is short, he knows he has to move fast.[36] As quickly as possible, Lucifer will implement a strategy that has been in his foul heart for ages. Keep in mind that Satan is not privy to God's prophetic timetable. He cannot possibly know the appointed timing of the rapture. He does not know the century, the decade, or the year it will take place. It is for this reason that he must have been grooming and preparing an antichrist *candidate* in every age. As such, we can be fairly confident that he has one waiting in the wings even now. And with the curtain drawn and the lights removed, the post-rapture world unknowingly awaits the unveiling of the man of sin upon the stage of humanity.

Of course, no one, including myself, knows exactly what will transpire in the hours, days, and months immediately following the rapture of the church. The scenarios I just described are certainly possible but they are not authoritative, prophetic, or binding. It may happen exactly as I have described. Or there could be some other national and global response that we have not considered or imagined.

Or it could be a whole lot worse.

Without being overly dramatic or speaking with too much hyperbole, even those familiar with last-days' prophecies are not prepared for the awful reality of a planet devoid of God's Spirit. In that day, the people of the earth will habitually hurl blasphemous curses at God, simultaneously experiencing an explosion of demonic worship, violence, and immorality. If all this is true (and it is), then perhaps *no* verbal scenario can adequately or sufficiently envision the darkness and decadence that will describe life in those coming days.

For decades, Americans feared world dictators, the Cold War, the nuclear threat, deadly pathogens, and now Islamic terrorism. Though all these threats have been real and viable, as it turns out, it's Jesus's rescue of His bride from a rebellious planet that will pull the pin, ignite public pandemonium, and usher in an unprecedented moment in human history.

And it could be the final act that ultimately causes America to breathe her last.

As the bride of Christ, we expectantly long for and anxiously await His return for us. But in the meantime, let us also *be* the church in our nation, holding back evil, prolonging America's heartbeat, and calling her toward repentance and salvation.

How Close Are We?

Precisely because we cannot predict the moment,
we must be ready at all moments.[1]

—C.S. Lewis

In this book, we have examined the current moral and spiritual condition of the United States. We have looked at how America has fallen into a sharp decline. We have retraced her roots and seen her original, historic connection to the values portrayed in holy Scripture. We have taken a detailed and uncensored look into some of her worst sins. We have exposed her pride and her stubborn refusal to submit to the God of heaven. We've discovered that, while our nation can ignore God, it will not be able to ignore the consequences of ignoring Him.

We have also walked through what Bible prophecy has to say about America's possible involvement in the end-times scenario we see depicted in God's Word. And we have taken into account what many believe to be the proverbial last straw, the prophetical event that catapults what's left of America into Revelation's day.

Granted, it has not always been a pleasant journey.

Hence, it should be fairly obvious by now that Bible prophecy is not some sort of Christian novelty. It is not a hobby for theological hermits, nor is it "leftover" truth for God's children to dive into if they are so inclined. To the contrary, prophecy is as much a part of the Word of God as the Psalms, Proverbs, the Gospels, or the epistles. Revelation is not the appendix of the Bible. It's the climax! And since as much as 28 percent of Scripture was prophetic at the time it was written, God must really want His children to be both informed and transformed by it.

There are those who feel we shouldn't study prophecy or teach and preach on it because there are just too many diverse interpretations and varying opinions concerning it. They see prophecy as more divisive than edifying. More confusing than comforting. Of course, you could say that about many Bible doctrines.

Others believe that none of us can really know what prophecy actually means. To them, it's too ethereal, vague, and cryptic. Too foggy and far off. Maybe even a bit irrelevant for daily Christian living.

I could not disagree more.

Many Christians feel that prophecy makes no sense down here, right now. That it doesn't really relate to our daily lives and where the world is now. But here and now is exactly where it makes the *most* sense. Prophecy is so much more then gaining facts or satisfying an itch to know what's going to happen in the future. It was meant for way more than that. More than simply giving us a heads up on history, prophecy gives us hope *today*. It gives us a unique perspective on the world in which we live, freeing us from the limitations and despair that characterizes many believers' lives in these last days. It strengthens our faith in both God and in His Word, inspiring us toward a different kind of life, one marked by purpose and destiny.

I acknowledge that many people are put off by the fact there are contrasting views regarding eschatology. But the fact that there is more than one eschatological perspective does not negate the fact that there is a correct view. And it in no way diminishes the role or importance prophecy plays in our lives today. Put simply, to ignore or avoid Bible prophecy and Revelation is to miss out on truth God has for us.

Instead of being ignored or minimized, prophecy should be engaged and embraced. It delivers critical truth about the future that impacts us right now. Just as the Old Testament prophets foresaw the day when Messiah would come and bring salvation to mankind, so God's people today must eagerly anticipate prophecies concerning His second coming and others not yet fulfilled.

Paul prophesied that in the last days, perilous times would come.[2] I believe we are living in those last days, and that the stage is being set for Bible prophecy to be fulfilled.

Even some in secular government understand we are living in a critical hour.

David Walker, a former US comptroller general, has said,

> There are striking similarities between America's current situation and the factors that brought down Rome, including declining moral values and political civility at home, an over-confident and over-extended military in foreign lands and fiscal irresponsibility by the central government.[3]

He also stated he believed our government was essentially on a "burning platform."

So in light of this and everything else we've seen in this book, we must ask: Just how close are we? How much longer until America fills up the "iniquity of the Amorites" and God sends His final judgment?[4] We've looked at the *who*, *what*, and *why* of America and Bible prophecy, but what about the *when*? Exactly when will these things take place? No one can say with 100 percent certainty, as we are unable to pinpoint the dates and times God has set for the future. We do not know when the clock will strike midnight, but we do know there is a clock. And that there is a midnight coming. Nevertheless, in the absence of a definitive time frame, we *can* still have an informed faith, and like the sons of Issachar, be people who "understand the times."[5]

While we have already considered that the next big prophetic event will be the rapture of the church, prophecy scholars hold varying views as to the timing of this event. Many, like myself, believe it will take place before the Tribulation (pre-Trib view). However, others see it as happening during the Tribulation (mid-Trib view).[6] A third view is that the rapture occurs at the end of the Tribulation (post-Trib). In this view, the rapture and second coming occur simultaneously.

But even with these contrasting perspectives, what virtually no eschatology expert will deny or dispute is that Jesus Christ *is* coming back and that evidence indicates we are indeed living in the last days. The fact that there are different views regarding the *timing* of last-days events does in no way negate the *reality* of them.

It's also important for us to understand that, from a spiritual point of view, America has been declining for decades. Though I believe the rapture will be the decisive chapter in America's downfall, other factors are currently contributing to our fall prior to that event. There's no way to definitively know how bad our economy will get before that critical moment, or if there'll be another major terror attack, or if some other national catastrophe will cripple us.

And exactly how bad will things get in the days leading up to the rapture? How severe will God's judgment become? What other foundational pillars supporting our country will crack or crumble?

What moral boundaries will be pushed, or even eliminated? How much worse can it get before we collapse from within? How far will America decline before experiencing her ultimate demise? Racing toward destruction, are we about to hit rock bottom? Every American who loves their country wants to know the answers to these questions.

There are, without a doubt, mysteries surrounding the end times. However, there are also many things we *do* know with certainty. It's the middle ground that sometimes trips us up—that place located somewhere between ignorance, knowledge, and pure guessing. Again, when studying or teaching Bible prophecy, we must avoid unfounded speculation and the trap of oversensationalizing the subject. These are the danger zones to dodge when speaking about the end times. We should not spend too much time looking for America in the Bible, but rather spend more time looking for ways to get the Bible to America. While we may not know the exact schedule of God's prophetic events or when America's decline will reach the point of no return, we can look and see what Scripture says about the signs that accompany the last days. Doing this won't provide exact dates for us, but it will give us a good idea of the *season* we are in.

So let's begin looking at some of those signs that Scripture says will characterize the final days of the church age.

Jesus, the "Doomsday Prophet"?

Anyone who reads the Gospels gains a panoramic perspective of Jesus and His earthly mission. Upon encountering His more memorable discourses and life scenes, the image of Christ most people walk away with is one of a loving and sacrificial Savior. And if that's been your experience, then you have correctly understood the Gospel writers' intent and message. But while this in an *accurate* assessment of the Son of God, it is not, however, a *complete* one.

In addition to sermons and stories regarding love, grace, and salvation, Jesus also brought truth about judgment, conflict, and coming wrath. A careful reading of the Gospels reveals that Jesus addressed uncomfortable and even disturbing topics. His language and communication style, while creative and relevant, was also direct and authoritative. And He left little doubt in His hearers' minds as to His motivation or meaning. Though not the whole of His ministry, there is no shortage of Christ's teachings on such controversial subjects as hell, sexual purity, self-discipline, divorce, shallow religiosity, hypocrisy, eternal damnation, and His exclusive right to deny heaven to anyone who refuses to trust in Him alone.[7]

Jesus Christ was the quintessential Truth Teller. Though popular with the masses for a while, they would eventually forsake Him. They discovered that the sword of His truth not only heals but also wounds those who encounter it. Jesus also ruffled the feathers of the Jewish spiritual elites, rebuking and even offending them. But whether welcomed and loved or rejected and hated, His character and content cut against the grain of conventional religion. He proclaimed a new, narrow way.[8]

Never one to waste words, the Carpenter from Nazareth declared with clarity God's unfiltered Word. He never backed down or apologized for His teachings, even when they angered the powers of His day. He had no aspirations of being a religious celebrity, and in fact, often retreated from the masses when necessary. He even thinned His own ranks at times…on purpose![9] I mean, what preacher does that? Clearly, the Son of God would not have competed well in today's high-profile, customer-driven Christian culture.

But to the point: Though Christ was not what we would call a prophet of doom, He nevertheless did not hesitate to speak prophetically concerning the future doom of planet earth—namely, the end times and coming judgment.

Jesus did more than just tell it like it is. He also told it like it *will be*. And what was future to His generation is becoming a present reality for us in ours.

In Matthew chapter 24, Jesus's disciples approached Him and asked a loaded question about the prophetic future: "Tell us, when will these things be, and what will be the sign of your coming, and of the end of the age?" (verse 3).

Jesus responded by launching into an apocalyptic discourse, giving them much of the content of Revelation, and profiling the Tribulation period. He outlined the biblical signs that will tell both the Jewish people and Tribulation believers that *the end of the end* is close at hand. He spoke of false prophets and counterfeit Christs. He prophesied of wars and rumors of wars, of an increase in famines and earthquakes, of murderous persecution, of lawlessness, and of the gospel being preached to the entire world.

Jesus also prophesied concerning the abomination of desolation, an event foretold by the prophet Daniel some 600 years before He was born. This horrifying incident will occur when Antichrist enters into the rebuilt Jewish temple in Jerusalem, declaring himself to be God and subsequently requiring the entire world to worship him. I believe this moment will happen at the midpoint of the Tribulation, and when it does, Jesus says to His kinsmen, "Drop everything, and run and hide." It is then that the man of sin will launch a concentrated campaign to annihilate every Jew on planet earth. Then Jesus concluded with the final sign of the end times—His second coming. This is when the Son of Man appears in the sky at Armageddon, and returns to earth.

Just like He said he would.

These are some of the things the Lord says will happen at "the end of the age" (and we know that these things have not already happened yet). So is there anything going on right now that tells us we are close to that time?

I believe the answer is yes.

Though these Tribulation signs have not yet become reality, there is strong evidence to indicate that the stage is being set for every one of them to come to pass, and perhaps soon.

Reading the Signs

Ours is an age of unprecedented technological advances and advantages. For example, the Internet offers a world of virtually unlimited knowledge at our fingertips 24/7. We can video chat in real time with someone on the other side of the world. Every day we are understanding more and more about the complexity of the universe and the human body. But one of my favorite technological tools is my phone's GPS, which I often use when I drive. I particularly appreciate how Siri can tell me what restaurants or gas stations are up ahead on my journey so that I can know what to look for. I love it that she can tell me how far away I am from my destination and *exactly* how long it will take me to there, down to the minute. This is so useful, because when you're traveling in unknown territory, it helps to have someone with you who knows what's up ahead and when you'll encounter it.

But can the Bible do that for us? Can Scripture tell us how long we have until we reach America's "final destination"? Jesus's disciples asked Him a similar question just prior to His ascension from the Mount of Olives. His response was, "It is not for you to know times or epochs which the Father has fixed by His own authority."[10]

Jesus went on to tell the disciples they should instead go back into Jerusalem and wait for the *next* prophetic sign to be fulfilled—the coming of the Holy Spirit.

Signs.

Of course, the trouble with signs is that they can be misread, misapplied, or just plain missed! At times, some in the prophecy community do just that—they misread, overspeculate, and thus miss the bull's-eye of God's truth. We must be careful not to present Bible prophecy in a way that capitalizes on people's curiosity or fear. And we should never exaggerate Scripture.

At the same time, we must not commit the error of scoffing at what Scripture clearly states will occur in the last days. Doing so blinds us from understanding the potential foreshadowing of those prophecies. The apostle Peter wrote that in the last days scoffers will arise, spouting their skepticism about the reality of Jesus's return (2 Peter 3:3-13). This is precisely what we see happening today when the subject of prophecy and the end times is brought up. We see this even in the body of Christ. I fear that the Western church has little to no regard for God's prophetic Word, and minimal training on how to discern the times in which we live. For when we dismiss or deny God's prophetic Word today, we commit the same error as those in Jesus's day. They failed to pay attention to the signs of His first coming, and as a result, they missed Him (Matthew 16:1-3).

We cannot ignore what Scripture clearly teaches, as Paul was adamant that believers not "be uninformed" about these things.[11] To knowingly ignore prophetic Scripture is to glory in our ignorance of the Word. And that would be a tragic mistake, for it plays right into the enemy's hands.

Therefore, to ask, "How close are we?" is a perfectly legitimate question. Prophecy matters. Then. Now. And in the days to come.

Bear in mind that God could fulfill all of Jesus's end-times prophecies without giving us *any* forewarning or previews. However, I believe He does give us some clues. Like a woman about to give birth to a child, America and the world are currently experiencing birth pangs. Contractions. Harrowing harbingers suggesting we are nearing the day of Revelation.

We have already established that the United States is nowhere specifically mentioned in Bible prophecy. We've also seen that the last pillar supporting America will be removed when Jesus returns for His bride. Beyond this point in time, it is unknown whether America will survive as other countries do in the Tribulation. It is possible that she will fade from history's headlines to become a mere back-page story. But since we're not there yet, is there anything taking place right now in our world that tells us we are close to witnessing the fulfillment of these prophecies?

Understand first of all that part of the nature of prophecy is that it is not always fully understood prior to its fulfillment. However, the closer you get to that fulfillment, the more in focus it usually becomes. Like a road sign that is hard to read from a distance, the nearer in proximity you are to it, the clearer it becomes. At other times, the Lord clears the fog at the last minute, enabling you to see what is up ahead or right in front of you. It is God's sovereign prerogative to determine how, when, and in what manner He reveals His prophecy's full meaning, timing, and fulfillment. And during those times when He chooses to keep us in the dark, we must trust in that which we *do* know from His Word.

Jesus began His Matthew 24 prophecies with a warning: "See to it that no one misleads you" (verse 4). He knows that others will come and distort both the Scriptures and reality itself, force-fitting them into their selfish agenda. So it is important, when approaching Bible prophecy, that we do so with careful discernment, distinguishing between truth and rumor, signs and speculation.

Because the rapture is imminent and inevitable, the end of America (as we know it) could occur at any moment. There are no specific prophetic signs that remain to be fulfilled before the rapture occurs.[12] It will just *happen*.

However, there *are* some stage-setting signs currently being fore-shadowed in our world today. And ultimately they affect all nations, America included. Jesus's prophecies and Revelation's realities are more likely to see their fulfillment in our lifetime than at any other time in the last 2000 years. Among them are:

Sign 1—The Jews Return Home to Their Promised Land

For Revelation's prophecies to unfold, Israel must be back in the land. In fact, many of the key events in the Bible's last book hinge on the existence of the nation Israel. The words of Jesus, John, and Daniel confirm this. We discussed this briefly back in chapter 3 when we talked about the Abrahamic covenant. This gathering is a *process*, like the bones in Ezekiel's vision coming together (Ezekiel 37). And this process has been going on for almost 130 years, begin-ning with the Zionist movement in the late 1800s. In all of human history, the Jews are the only exiled race to remain a distinct people. This, despite being scattered to more than 70 countries for more than 2000 years. Egypt, Assyria, Babylon, Persia, Greece, and Rome all conquered the Jewish nation, took their land and people cap-tive, and ultimately dispersed them throughout the earth. And they continued being persecuted down through the ages. And yet amaz-ingly, on May 14, 1948, Israel officially became a nation again. As a result of this prophetic miracle, more Jews are living in Israel today than at any time since Jesus walked the earth. If you want to keep your finger on the pulse of end-times prophecy, keep your eyes on Israel. The Old Testament prophets foresaw this day when the Jews would return to the land.[13] Their return has been called a "super sign" of prophecy. It is *the* sign of the last days, and it is happening right before our very eyes.

Sign 2—Israel Is Invaded by a Surrounding Coalition of Hostile Nations

This prophetic event is popularly known as the Battle of Gog and Magog (Ezekiel 38–39), which I mentioned back in chapter 6. The goal of these nations is to eradicate Israel, and the coalition will be spearheaded by Russia and an alliance of Muslim nations, many of whom are currently salivating at the prospect of destroying Israel.

In recent years, Russia has been positioning itself militarily in this region, establishing a strong (and seeming permanent) presence in Syria. Combat helicopters, tanks, armored personnel carriers, and surface-to-air missiles are all stationed there, helping Syria fight ISIS as well as preserving the current Bashar al-Assad regime.[14] This move by Russia is simply part of the chess pieces presently being put into place for what the Bible says will be an eventual invasion.

I find it more than just coincidence that the prophesied nations who will come against Israel with Russia are overwhelmingly Muslim.[15] And the reason we know this battle is still future is because there was never an invasion of Israel like this in the Old Testament, and there could *not* have been one over the last 2000 years because there was no Israel!

As to the timing of this particular battle, I believe there is scriptural evidence to suggest it will occur sometime *after* Israel enters the land and *before* Jesus Christ returns. More specifically, the Bible tells us it will take place during the "latter years" and when Israel is "living securely" in the land (Ezekiel 38:8,11,14,18-22). The encirclement of Israel by these Muslim countries and the movement by Russia to become more militarily dominant in the region suggest that they are ramping up to this epic battle (which, by the way, Israel will win).[16] The rise of radical Islam, ISIS, and anti-Semitism in these last days may point toward a time when the majority of the Muslim world will finally unite and move against Israel. Jesus was right—there will be "wars and rumors of wars" (Matthew 24:6).

Sign 3—Antichrist Brokers a Peace Treaty with Israel (Daniel 9:27; Revelation 6:1-2; 1 Thessalonians 5:1-3)

The designated time frame for this treaty is seven years, and the signing of it is what officially signals the beginning of the Tribulation.[17] For the "abomination of desolation" Jesus spoke of to occur, the Jewish temple has to be rebuilt (see Sign 4). And in order for that to happen, this strategic peace agreement must somehow help facilitate Israel in retaking the Temple Mount, or at least a part of it. Right now, tensions in the Middle East are high. We are but one devastating rocket strike away from another war in that region. Every American president in recent history has made attempts to bring peace to that region. But all have failed. Antichrist will not. Even today if some world leader were to mastermind a peace accord between Israel and her enemies, he would win the Nobel Peace Prize and be hailed as a Messiah-like figure, having been able to do what no political figure has ever done.

Sign 4—The Jewish Temple Is Rebuilt in Jerusalem (Daniel 9:27; Matthew 24:15; 2 Thessalonians 2:3-4)

Remember, there hasn't been a temple in Jerusalem since AD 70, when the Roman general Titus sacked and subdued Jerusalem, destroying the temple. Jesus prophesied about the temple's destruction in Matthew 24:1-2. In fact, it was this discussion that prompted the disciples to ask Him what the signs of the end times would be. But today, Israel is once again a nation and millions of Jews have returned, and a movement toward rebuilding their temple has officially begun.

In 1987, an organization called the Temple Institute was formed in anticipation of the time when the practice of traditional worship and sacrifice would be rebirthed for the Jewish people. This organization has already fashioned sacred temple vessels and priestly garments according to exact Old Testament specifications. They have also founded a training institute for temple priests, and have already begun reinstituting the ceremonial practice of animal sacrifices, just as they did in the Old Testament. All this is happening right now. They're simply waiting for some way (i.e., a peace treaty) to secure the spot on the Temple Mount so that construction can begin on the new temple.

Sign 5—Apostasy (1 Timothy 4:1-3; 2 Timothy 3:1-3; 2 Peter 2:1-22; 3:3-6; Jude 1-25)

Both during the Tribulation and leading up to it, there will be a falling away from the faith. The word *apostasy* means to "depart" or "fall away." There are both similarities and differences between what that apostasy looks like now and during the Tribulation. What we are seeing today is a surge of apostasy in America's churches and Christian universities where the authority of God's Word is being undermined. And in recent years, there has been an explosion of "Christian" authors and bloggers who have made all sorts of extra-biblical claims. They have also captivated the minds of many undiscerning believers. This is the kind of false teaching about which Paul warned Timothy.[18]

Though not characteristic of all, some of these bloggers and authors have gathered for themselves huge followings, establishing sentimental connections with them over subjects such as marriage, parenting, and faith-based issues. Using their high-profile position, they then cross over into the world of biblical truth, espousing heretical teachings about supposed visits to heaven, reimagining sexuality and relationships, and the heresy of universalism. The result is that they are leading many people astray while unknowingly condemning themselves. These self-appointed Bible teachers are, as Paul declared, peddlers of the Word,[19] having departed from the truth both doctrinally and morally.

Concerning this last-days apostasy, Dr. Dwight Pentecost wrote, "This open deliberate willful repudiation of the truth of the Bible is described in scripture as one of the major characteristics of the last days of the church on earth."[20]

Just as Satan did in the Garden of Eden, these professing Christians doubt, question, and even deny core teachings of Scripture. Sometimes subtly, and other times overtly, they alter truth and redefine biblical values (like love, grace, acceptance) to fit their own theology and personal preferences. Dr. Mark Hitchcock and I have written a book specifically addressing this subject. Titled *The Coming Apostasy*, in it we detail how this departure from the faith is occurring in our country, how it's affecting the average Christian, how to recognize it, and what can be done about it.

But what we are seeing right now is only a preview of the final apostasy that will occur during the Tribulation. In that heretical hour, "Judas Christians" will fall away from the faith, betraying those who have genuinely come to faith in Jesus and delivering them up to death (Mathew 24:10-12).

Sign 6—*The World Moves Toward Globalism*

The international community is connected today like no other time in history. Nationalism and patriotism are on the decline, while being a "world citizen" is becoming more en vogue. A move to "erase all borders" is gaining popularity, particularly with millennials. Countries are coming together, whether it be for political, trade, or financial reasons.

Much of this is being driven by Satan, who has always sought a world united under his rule. Revelation 17 describes a revived Roman Empire that will form in the end times. Comprised of ten major nations, this empire will become Antichrist's symbolic scepter. The current European Union, or some form of it, *could* be a foreshadowing of such a global alliance. Right now, there is so much interdependence between nations that if one were to collapse financially, it would greatly impact all the others.[21] Of course, the global trauma brought on by the rapture of the church will rapidly accelerate the convergence of nations together toward the common goal of survival.

There are additional prophecies in Revelation being foreshadowed now as well. For example, it is now technologically possible to mark humanity with a universal brand, without which they can neither buy nor sell.[22] This "mark of the beast" is no longer science fiction, but rather a present possibility. Whether it takes the form of RFID (Radio Frequency Identification), an implant about the size of a grain of rice, or some other more primitive method, it will become an economic necessity when the post-rapture global financial crisis hits.

Scripture also prophesies that when Jesus Christ returns to this world, His feet will touch the Mount of Olives, causing a massive, violent earthquake that splits the Mount east to west, moving it north to south.[23] As reported by NBC News in 2004, a study by the Geological Survey of Israel confirmed the Mount of Olives to be at *imminent* risk for an earthquake, as geologists have located a fault line that runs right through the Mount…you guessed it, east to west.[24]

God isn't teasing us with these prophecies, my friend. Instead, He's *telling* us what's going to happen. So far, His Word's prophetic track record is perfect. Not even one of the prophecies foretold by

Scripture has failed to come to pass. If the Author of History says it's going to happen, you can bank on it.

I believe we will continue seeing the floodwaters of ungodliness rise in America as we race toward Revelation. Expect to experience further aftershocks from the legalization of homosexual marriages and the collapse of our moral levees. We must not naïvely think that simply allowing legal unions for homosexuals is the end of Satan's immoral agenda. Regardless of who occupies the Oval Office, I believe there will be a continued increase of hostility toward Bible-believing Christians and the values we espouse. Globally speaking, we will likely see more regional conflicts, more sword-rattling between nations, and the ongoing threat of war.

The Last Breath?

To be clear, these signs do not mean the rapture, Revelation, and the Tribulation will happen tomorrow. However, they do signify that the conditions are right for the storm to make landfall. And it does appear the stage is being set for history's final drama. Understandably, the question on everyone's mind is this: When? And again, Jesus gives us guidance in navigating these choppy waters.

When the Pharisees and Sadducees approached Him to ask that He show them a supernatural sign from heaven, He rebuked them, saying,

> When evening comes, you say, "It will be fair weather, for the sky is red," and in the morning, "Today it will be stormy, for the sky is red and overcast." You know how to interpret the appearance of the sky, but *you cannot interpret the signs of the times.* A wicked and adulterous generation looks for a sign, but none will be given it except the sign of Jonah.[25]

These religious leaders were so obsessed with looking for super-natural signs that they could not see the signs of the times happening right in front of them! Rather than frantically digging through headlines looking for clues, we should look to God's Word, which is both our greatest sign and sign-explainer.

There are those today who see signs everywhere, embedded in some secret conspiracy or hidden in every major world event. But we must not be taken in by every end-times theory or succumb to the faulty forecasts offered by speculators. Instead, we must firmly tether our hearts and minds to the Bible. God's Word is our only real authority and GPS on this prophetic journey. When we depart from Scripture, we quickly move from biblical signs to sensationalism and senseless speculation. The signs I've mentioned to you in this chapter tell us that current world conditions clearly support and complement Scripture's predictions. Even so, we must be patient and have faith in God's sovereign and wise plan for the ages.

For more than 30 years, I served as a pastor. During that time, I made numerous visits to dying church members in hospitals, nursing homes, and hospices during the final hours of their lives. Many times prior to entering the room, a doctor or family member would take me aside to give me their thoughts or prognosis on how much time they estimated the patient had left. Sometimes upon seeing the physical condition of the person, it became obvious to me that they were not long for this world. I've prayed with dying saints who had only days or even hours to live. However, on the other hand, I've also seen others miraculously rebound, regain their strength, and live a lot longer than anyone expected or predicted.

As a nation, America is a living thing. She was conceived and born in time. She has survived for almost 250 years through wars and economic collapses. She has been vibrant, a land of freedom and opportunity for all who found her. And she has been a beacon of hope for the nations. She has been divided internally, and at times wrought with political, racial, economic, and moral tension and unrest. She has been viciously attacked and yet fought, survived, and returned to her former strength and glory. She has battled injustice and tyranny across the world, and sacrificed her sons on foreign soil for the sake of freedom. She has flourished and made herself rich and affluent, becoming the envy of nations. Through weakness and adversity, she has persevered, defied the odds, and survived longer than many expected.

But along the way, America forgot God. Having been built on a solid foundation of Judeo-Christian values, she failed to remain anchored to those principles. Like Israel of old, she ignored warnings from God's messengers to forsake her sin and tear down her altars of idolatry. As a result, God has now turned her over to her own desires. Sadly, this country is under the sentence of divine judgment. As a nation, we are on death row, though the date of our ultimate end is not yet known.

The question now is this: Is it possible to turn this country around? Or is it too late for America? Have we passed the point of no return? Are we doomed without any chance of reprieve? Is a miraculous midnight-hour pardon even possible? Could there yet be a final awakening? In light of our country's condition, what are we as Christians supposed to do?

What *can* we do?

A Time for Christians to Rise

Never lose heart in the power of the gospel.

—Charles Spurgeon

In my home study is a unique artifact prominently displayed on a bookshelf. Surrounded by commentaries and works of theology, this antique curio seems a bit out of place. It is 9 x 11 inches, made entirely of steel, shaped like a pot, and is a faded olive-drab color. The treasured possession I'm describing is an Army helmet from World War II. I purchased it from an elderly shopkeeper in Bayeux, France, a few years ago while on an anniversary trip with my wife. The Normandy area visit was one of my "bucket list" items. It had always been my dream to visit the D-Day beaches and walk in the footsteps of the men whom I regard as heroes.

When I bought this particular souvenir, the aged shop owner explained how the helmet had only recently been dug up, having been buried in the Normandy mud for over 65 years. Remarkably, it's in fairly good shape, though it bears the scars of time. It is unknown whether the pointed indentations on it are the result of ground pressure or bullet impacts. Any identifiable markings that once decorated the Army-green steel are long gone, and all that's left behind is a tangible relic of the military campaign that saved the world.

Cleaned up and mounted on a special stand, it now sits as a silent sentry, a tattered testament to an era long since passed. I've often wondered what story that helmet could tell. Was it blown off a paratrooper's head while he hastily jumped from a C-47 airplane in the predawn hours of D-Day? Did it tumble from a wounded soldier, who stumbled to the ground after being shot? Was it blasted off of the man it once protected due to a German grenade or mortar fire? And what about the young man who wore that helmet? Why did he leave it behind? Did he eventually make it home alive from the war to feel the loving embrace of his parents? Or was his lifeless body later returned stateside? Could what remains of him, like the helmet he once wore, still be entombed somewhere in the Normandy countryside?

I will never know the answers to those questions. But this I do know: Whoever once wore that helmet was an American, and part of the Greatest Generation. Theirs was a time in history when millions of young men volunteered to fight for their country and to rid the world of a great evil. And more than 400,000 of America's sons gave their lives in that global conflict. I am also pretty sure that whoever this young man was, even though he was fighting for a just cause, in his heart he just wanted to go home.

I love my country.

And I have always felt privileged and proud to call myself an American.

I make no apologies for that in a global climate where nationalism is frowned upon. There have been moments when that love for country has overwhelmed me. As a young boy, I sat before a black-and-white television on July 20, 1969, and watched in wide-eyed wonder as Neil Armstrong become the first human to set foot on the moon. Like many, I have witnessed the somber changing of the guard at the Tomb of the Unknown Soldier in Washington, DC. I have walked the rows of crosses at Arlington and at the American cemetery at Colleville-sur-Mer overlooking Omaha Beach, where thousands of young hero soldiers are interred. They gave all their *tomorrows* so we could enjoy all our *todays*.

My firstborn son is a graduate of the US Military Academy at West Point. He became a part of the Long Gray Line knowing full well he could one day be asked to lay down his life for his country. In my many visits to that prestigious school during his four years there, I never got over the depth of history housed within those storied stone-grey buildings. Situated on the picturesque Hudson River in upstate New York, it's at West Point where George Washington once marched his troops, and where America's legendary military leaders were formed and forged. Names like Davis, Lee, Grant, Jackson, Pershing, Patton, MacArthur, and Eisenhower read like a "Who's Who" of American history.

Pardon my patriotism, but there's nothing like being an American.

Every July 4, our country is repainted red, white, and blue for a day. We pause from our busy schedules to celebrate with flame-grilled burgers, family gatherings, and fireworks. And what could possibly equal the unifying resolve we felt after Pearl Harbor or in the days following the 9/11 attacks? What can match hearing 50,000 voices sing the national anthem at a major league baseball game?

Yes, I am both grateful and proud to be an American.

However, as wonderful and inspiring as this is, being a citizen of this country is not my highest privilege or my primary identity. Being a child of God *is*. One is earthly, the other heavenly. One temporal, the other eternal. And because of this, my greatest and highest loyalty lies with another kingdom, a kingdom whose coming Jesus asked us to pray for.[1]

Heavenly-Minded

After more than 30 years of pastoral leadership and speaking to churches across this country, it has become apparent to me that we in the American church have lost a fundamental perspective. It's a flaw in our collective faith that must be corrected. Our problem is that we think and act like we actually *belong* here. Like this earth is our home. Yes, we currently live here, but according to the Bible, we as Christians also enjoy a unique dual citizenship. As Paul reminded the Philippian believers, "Our citizenship is in heaven, from which also we eagerly wait for a Savior, the Lord Jesus Christ" (3:20).

This truth is more than just a comforting thought or a trendy Christian meme. It's a theological reality concerning our ultimate destiny. Recognizing this priority of citizenship means acknowledging our membership in an eternal kingdom. It's a citizenship that comes with inherent privileges and responsibilities. It means that heaven, not this world, is where our primary allegiance lies.

It means we don't belong here.

And when this truth kicks in, we feel an inner tug of our hearts heavenward. Like the pull that the Holy Land exerts on the Jews who are returning there, for us there is an invisible pull toward a city "whose architect and builder is God."[2] It means, like the soldier who once strapped on that helmet on display in my study, we long to go home.

However, we're not home—yet. Even so, something inside us yearns for the day when Jesus will return. For Paul, this eternal perspective of our heavenly citizenship carried eschatological expectations. Concerning this, the apostle wrote to the Colossians,

> If you have been raised up with Christ, keep seeking the
> things above, where Christ is, seated at the right hand of
> God. *Set your mind on the things above*, not on the things
> that are on earth. For you have died and your life is hid-
> den with Christ in God. When Christ, who is our life,
> is revealed, then you also will be revealed with Him in
> glory (3:1-4).

Though we are often mired in the mud of earthly necessities, Paul urges us to order our priorities. It's not that things down here are unimportant. It's just that they are not of the *utmost* importance. This means there is something more essential and satisfying then making money. Something more compelling than watching college football. Something more important than gymnastics, little league baseball games, friendships, dating, or keeping house. Something more beneficial than getting an education or landing that dream job. Something even more worthwhile then a well-deserved vacation, a good family, or a great marriage.

Something even better than sex.

Though all of the above are good things and gifts from God, and though they all have their merit and place here on earth, nothing compares to that which is heavenly. And do you know why? Paul tells us it's because our "life [our true, new self and destiny] is hid-den with Christ in God."

We belong to *Him*. His presence is our pursuit and His king-dom our cause. And the key to cementing this perspective into our lives is to "*set* our minds." In other words, to keep seeking the things above and to focus on them. To "keep seeking" means to actively pursue something. When Jesus was addressing the issue of earthly necessities and concerns (food, drink, clothing), He exhorted His disciples to *seek* first the kingdom of God, and all of these other earthly requirements would fall naturally into place.[3] Contrary to conventional thinking, the things that give us life and fulfillment are not the things this world can give. At times we may wonder why we are experiencing so much stress and anxiety. Some of that anxiety stems from placing certain earthly priorities above heavenly ones. Being more preoccupied with work, hobbies, leisure, family, spouse, or self than with God is a recipe for worry, sorrow, and depression.[4]

If you really want anxiety, try putting God second…or fifth. Jesus wasn't inferring that earthly concerns were unimportant or that we should not seek them. He simply wanted us to know that God's concerns should be sought *first*. It's how we were designed to function. It's also, incidentally, what brings us the greatest joy, peace, and fulfillment. That's what Paul meant by "keep seeking"—you are to actively pursue heavenly things as your number one priority. Seeking is a choice every believer can freely make. It's an act made by a will that has been freed from sin's bondage by Jesus's redeeming power.

But then the apostle follows that command with another. With the heart/soul we seek, but with the mind, we *think*. To "set your mind on the things above" means that godly, eternal values are to preoccupy your thoughts. This does *not* mean that we should become like monks and retreat to the confines of a monastery, where all we do is contemplate Scripture all day. Again, the ordering of priorities is what Paul, like Jesus, had in mind here. He was saying you are to "put your mind where Christ is."

Is Jesus concerned about things on earth? Yes. Is He working through His Spirit here? Yes. But His highest objective is to one day bring glory to the Father by fulfilling His promise to His children and by causing His kingdom to come. Jesus's focus while on earth was to accomplish the mission for which He was sent.[5] And He accomplished that mission.[6]

But how? By setting His heart and mind on things above

(heavenly, spiritual priorities). That's how He was able to "resolutely set out for Jerusalem" (Luke 9:51 NIV). Jesus Christ came to die for us, and what motivated Him to endure the cross, despise the shame, and suffer such an ignominious death was a joy awaiting Him in heaven.[7] That heavenly joy was bringing glory to the Father, and bringing salvation to those who would believe.

So this eternal perspective to which we are called and commanded supersedes and overrules all temporary priorities. It trumps earthly pursuits and outranks human obligations.[8] It means we see ourselves as what we actually are—first and foremost, *disciples*. Children. Followers. Worshippers. Servants of the Most High God. "Aliens and strangers" in a foreign land.[9] This is our *identity*. Our blood-bought eternal reality. It is only when we view ourselves in this manner that we can truly appreciate, pursue, and properly steward the privilege of being Christians in a country like America.

This is Paul's main motivation behind his earlier words to the Philippians:

> To me, to live is Christ and to die is gain. But if I am to live on in the flesh, this will mean fruitful labor for me; and I do not know which to choose. But I am hard-pressed from both directions, having the desire to depart and be with Christ, for that is very much better; yet to remain on in the flesh is more necessary for your sake (1:21-24).

The apostle often experienced the tension that exists between wanting to stay here and help others and to simply go on to be with Christ. Every true believer does.

Nineteenth-century poet Oliver Wendell Holmes famously said, "Some people are so heavenly minded that they are no earthly good." I have heard Christians quote this, as if setting your mind on spiritual truth was somehow a bad thing. However, as Christians, we often model just the opposite, being so "earthly minded that we are no *heavenly* good." But it's not a matter of either/or, as if everything on earth is inherently opposed to everything in heaven. Rather, it's a matter of *heart values*. God wants us to be *more* heavenly minded than to allow earthly necessities to dictate our affections and actions. And it is not just a matter of simply putting more man-hours and thought time into godly things than we do secular ones. It is not a time-measurement issue. That kind of paint-by-number, measurable Christianity only leads to legalism, which actually feeds the sin nature. Instead, it's a priority or value issue.

I have striven to always make my family a greater and higher priority to me than my ministry. As my sons grew up, they knew this. Though I was far from a perfect father to them, they knew that they outranked my job at the church. I demonstrated this to them by turning down speaking engagements or curtailing church activities in order to be at home or be with them. However, that fixed priority did not mean I thought *more* about them during an eight-hour workday at the church office than I did my ministry responsibilities. More actual minutes were spent studying, counseling, and discipling. Even so, my family still outranked my commitment to the church.

Being heavenly minded means God's values, as portrayed in Scripture outrank earthly pursuits, pleasures, and priorities. In reality, the Christian who is heavenly minded actually does *more* earthly good than those whose primary allegiance lies with this world!

So the first thing we as Christians must do is to *renew* our perspective concerning our identity and our destiny. Then we must *reorder* our priorities to reflect that present and future reality.

Choose Wisely

Having now contemplated America's decline and moral demise, we who follow Jesus Christ have some decisions to make. The first choice we must make is the personal one we just discussed. As with every true change, it must begin internally, with the heart. But this concentric circle of change emanates outward, and must also encompass the Christian church corporately. It is here where there are options and paths before us. Some of these paths are more beneficial than others to our present country and to God's future kingdom. So what are we to do in response to *The End of America?* I see five possible paths before us.

First, we can run and retreat. Simply withdraw from culture, removing all godly influence and voice in society. We could call it "rapture practice," in anticipation of the time when the Holy Spirit's restraining power and influence will be taken out of the way. This choice effectively removes the light, completely conceding and surrendering to the darkness and evil that threatens us. Government, education, science, the arts, sports, literature, and media would all be handed over to whoever and whatever is left behind in the black void. We disengage ourselves from society, preventing our children from having contact with any who are "not like us." This option, of course, is not only unthinkable but also unbiblical, as Jesus has purposely placed us in the world for His cause (Matthew 5:17; John 17:15). We are here "*in the midst* of a crooked and perverse generation, among whom you appear as lights in the world" (Philippians 2:15). We are not here to conform to the world, but rather to transform it while remaining distinct from it.[10]

Option number two, we can condemn everything. This option relates to the first, though we would still maintain a voice in culture, albeit one heard from a distance. Here, we criticize and denounce

America from afar while simultaneously lobbing "gospel grenades" from within the safe and secure confines of the church walls. Adopting this strategy means we don't really care if America survives or if people are actually saved. We're just glad *we* made it to spiritual safety in time before the big one hits. From a purely practical standpoint, this approach (which is employed by many Christians) is woefully ineffective to cause any real change or help anyone spiritually. What many may not realize is that nonbelievers really don't care what Christians think about them. They are so absorbed in themselves and in earthly pursuits that our spiritual salvos have no effect on them other than to perpetuate a stereotype of religious bigotry and further justify their hatred of us.

In reality, the life-changing gospel of Jesus Christ and His truth is best delivered up close and personal, and always accompanied by love, humility, dignity, and gentleness.[11] Yes, there are definitely times to call out a culture and a country with regard to sin. That's part of what this book does. However, truth that is divorced from hope and love is really nothing more than cold, condemning, sterile facts. We must resist this option.

A third path we could choose is to simply remain absorbed in our Christian subculture. The American evangelical church excels at keeping believers occupied with Christian "stuff." We have become experts at staying busy "doing church." This is where things get a bit tricky. I mean, didn't Paul say to "set your mind on the things above"? If so, then what's wrong with Christian activities, ministries, programs, and alternative holiday events (code-named "evangelistic outreaches") that keep Christians separate from the world while inviting non-Christians into the church? That's a *good* thing, right?

We must first note that there is not a single Bible verse that tells Christians to bring non-Christians to church so that they can "get saved." Not one. Second, remember what we said about time versus priorities? Simply adding up the amount of time we spend doing something doesn't automatically equate to that something being the most important thing in our lives. The same is true with Christian activities. Satan does not care how many activities we sponsor within the walls of our church. Filling our calendars with church stuff is not necessarily an indication of Christian maturity or advanced spirituality. It may only mean you do a lot of church activities. This is an area where wisdom is needed. Just because an activity or event is Christian in nature doesn't mean it's something a Christian should do.

A fundamental struggle we're experiencing in the Western church world is that many pastors have departed from the primary biblical mandate to equip the saints for the work of service (Ephesians 4:11-14.) Instead of focusing on teaching sound doctrine and deepening believers in their faith, we're creating and designing church services and ministries that cater to a consumer-driven Christian populace.[12]

The church has become Walmart.

While conservative Christians criticize a welfare state government and those who live off governmental assistance, we are not far from the same when we expect the institutional church to provide for our every need. When "shopping" for churches, the consumer-driven Christian expects there to be a ministry for every age group and season of life. And it's not just spiritual provision that we require. We are also expecting the church to meet our social needs as well, providing friendships and social gathering opportunities.

There are even some who expect the church should meet their physical needs, providing athletic facilities, gymnasiums (we call them family life centers) and sports leagues. In thinking that we are ministering to the total person, we end up creating a subculture in which we effectively remove ourselves from the world.

As we live in a worldly culture where marketing is all about making people feel good about themselves and meeting their needs, the church must fight against becoming just another place where "customers" can come, consume, and make a payment. This is a sure sign that the bride has lost her first love, and that she is in danger of having Jesus remove her influence and effectiveness in the world.[13] Just because a church does a lot of things doesn't mean that church is alive. In fact, it may demonstrate just the opposite.[14]

Fourth, we can choose to be absorbed by culture. Because the church is obviously not making progress in holding back the floodwaters of sin in our country, should we simply adopt the old adage "If you can't beat 'em, join 'em"? In light of the overwhelming surge of sin and the undercurrent of anti-Christian thought in our society, should we stop swimming upstream and just go with the flow? It seems clear at this stage that we are not going to win this war, so why even try?

This defeatist attitude has no place in a Christian's mind, as John reminds us: "Greater is He who is in you than he who is in the world," and "Whatever is born of God overcomes the world; and this is the victory that has overcome the world—our faith. Who is the one who overcomes the world, but he who believes that Jesus is the son of God?"[15]

While we might not understand all of God's purposes in allowing evil to exist and prevail, we do know that one day He *will* put an end to it all. When the last chapter of history is written, we will be the victors! Jesus reminds us, "These things I have spoken to you, so that in Me you may have peace. In the world you have tribulation, but take courage; *I have overcome the world*" (John 16:33).

But there is a fifth and final path that lies before us. And it's the one I believe God wants His people to take. While we eagerly anticipate the return of Jesus Christ to rescue His bride from the wrath to come, we must not only focus on what we are to *do*, but also realize who we are to *be*. The apostle James urged us to "be doers of the word, and not merely hearers who delude themselves."[16] The sin of hearing but not doing is as bad as knowing but not being. In other words, we cannot really do what God has asked us to do unless we first become the Christians He wants us to be.

We are a redeemed, blood-bought people—washed clean of all sin, forgiven, made righteous in the Father's sight, freed from condemnation, sealed by the Holy Spirit, beloved of God, the apple of His eye, empowered by His Spirit, commissioned by His Son, entrusted with the truth and the treasure of the gospel of Jesus Christ, and commanded to *penetrate* our culture and the darkness that defines it.

This is who we are. And this is what we must do.

So what will *you* do?

If the church would just *be* the church, we could make a tangible difference in our country.

An old proverb says, "It's better to light a candle than to curse the darkness." A quaint saying, but the Bible states this principle more authoritatively.

Jesus said, "I am the light of the world. Whoever follows me will never walk in darkness, but will have the light of life" (John 8:12 NIV), and "I have come into the world as a light, so that no one who believes in me should stay in darkness" (12:46 NIV).

To His disciples, Jesus proclaimed, "You are the light of the world. A city set on a hill cannot be hidden" (Matthew 5:14).

And to the church, Paul declared, "For at one time you were darkness, but now you are light in the Lord. Walk as children of light" (Ephesians 5:8 ESV).

To the Romans, Paul added a note of urgency to this command, writing, "The night is almost gone, and the day is near. Therefore, let us lay aside the deeds of darkness and put on the armor of light" (Romans 13:12).

As you already know, there is risk involved with "being the light." Just after telling Nicodemus that "God so loved the world," Jesus said, "This is the judgment: the light has come into the world, and people loved the darkness rather than the light because their works were evil" (John 3:16,19 ESV).

As we've seen, light illumines. It brings both knowledge and comfort. But it also exposes, and is often unwelcome, especially to those accustomed to living in the dark.

Sometimes prophetic calls to repentance fall on deaf ears and defiant hearts. But our job is not to determine the response to the light, but rather, to faithfully shine it in the darkness. If you love your country like you say you do, then be the church and shine the light of the gospel wherever you are.

A Final Call

Often at Christian rallies where speakers talk about being a Christian influence in our secular culture, someone will inevitably read 2 Chronicles 7:14:

> [If] My people who are called by My name humble themselves and pray and seek My face and turn from their wicked ways, then I will hear from heaven, will forgive their sin and will heal their land.

The problem with citing this passage in relation to America is that God spoke this promise specifically to Solomon, the king of *Israel.* These words were *for* Israel with a specific context in mind. The occasion was the dedication of the first temple. The healing of the land, then, refers specifically to bringing physical rain to prevent crop failure. It's not talking about spiritual restoration. Those words weren't spoken so that one day they might be used for political purposes or for Christians to pull out when they talk about trying to fix America's problems. God is speaking about "My people," or Israel, and not America. And "land" doesn't refer to the United States.

Second Chronicles 7:14 is not a promise of revival in America, nor is it a call for America to return to God, though as individual Americans, we desperately need to humble ourselves and repent. It is a verse that addresses Israel, illegitimately used and ripped from its context for dramatic effect. America is not the church, nor is she Israel. In our self-centric age, we often forget that not everything in the Bible is about us. We can't take a promise made to Israel for a specific context and time, and magically make it about America. Spiritualizing or making allegories out of Scripture passages dishonors God's Word and cheats us out of its true meaning.

So why drastically misinterpret and misapply an Old Testament verse when the New Testament has already given us specific instructions about bringing salvation and healing to our country? Jesus has already told us to "make disciples of all the nations."[17] While America did not exist when Jesus made that statement, He did intend for His church to spread throughout the entire world, encompassing persons "from every tribe and tongue and people and nation."[18]

And that *does* include the United States of America.

If you want to find America in the Bible, look no further than the Great Commission. My friend, economic prosperity will not save us. Democrats or Republicans cannot save us. A good or patriotic president, though needed and welcomed, cannot save us. What ultimately happens to America prior to the rapture transcends political parties and their abilities to legislate laws, implement or cut programs, or bring about reform. Ours is a *spiritual* problem requiring a spiritual solution. And until we recognize this, the only kind of change that really matters remains a distant hope.

I am not sure America the country can be saved, but I am quite sure that Americans can.

Many pastors, leaders, and individuals are praying for a national revival. And one may indeed come, though it is nowhere prophesied in Scripture. What *is* prophesied is a last-days apostasy, or falling away from the faith.[19] This is why we must be sure to guard our hearts and help other believers around us to remain faithful to God and the pure teaching of His Word. For if the church succumbs to apostasy, there is certainly no chance for revival.

Therefore, now is the time for Christians to rise. Not next year. Not next week. But *now*. If there is to be any real hope and reformation for these United States, let it begin right now. And let it begin with *me*. And *you*.

In 1940, during the early months of World War II, Adolf Hitler's armies conquered Holland, Luxembourg, and Belgium. Within the span of one week in June of that year, Paris fell, and France surrendered to Germany. All the world knew that England was next on Hitler's evil agenda, and that the German war machine would soon invade the shores of that nation. On June 18 of that same year, British prime minister Winston Churchill spoke to the House of Commons concerning the disastrous turn of events in Europe. Realizing Britain now stood alone against Hitler's military, and that the prospect of years of war lay ahead of them, the prime minister delivered what would become one of the most inspiring speeches of the twentieth century. He concluded it with these words:

> What General Weygand called the Battle of France is over. I expect that the Battle of Britain is about to begin. Upon this battle depends the survival of Christian civilization. Upon it depends our own British life, and the long continuity of our institutions and our Empire. The whole fury and might of the enemy must very soon be

turned on us. Hitler knows that he will have to break us in this Island or lose the war. If we can stand up to him, all Europe may be free and the life of the world may move forward into broad, sunlit uplands. But if we fail, then the whole world, including the United States, including all that we have known and cared for, will sink into the abyss of a new Dark Age made more sinister, and perhaps more protracted, by the lights of perverted science. Let us therefore brace ourselves to our duties, and so bear ourselves that, if the British Empire and its Commonwealth last for a thousand years, men will still say, "This was their finest hour."[20]

A generation earlier, a Presbyterian clergyman named William Pierson Merrill wrote a hymn calling the church to embrace its godly priorities and responsibilities. Originally titled "Rise Up, O Men of God," the classic hymn has sometimes substituted "saints" in place of "men" in order to include the whole church. Merrill's words are more prophetically relevant today than ever before:

> Rise up, O saints of God!
> Have done with lesser things;
> Give heart and mind and soul and strength
> To serve the King of kings.
> Rise up, O saints of God!
> His kingdom tarries long;
> Bring in the day of brotherhood
> And end the night of wrong.
> Rise up, O saints of God!
> The Church for you doth wait,
> Her strength unequal to her task,

Rise up, and make her great!
Lift high the cross of Christ!
Tread where His feet have trod;
As foll'wers of the Son of Man,
Rise up, O Church of God!

God is calling His people to rise up, stand strong, and move forward, knowing that nothing we do in His Spirit and for His name is ever wasted.[21] We as American Christians must fight for our country while simultaneously helping to stem the tide of sin, pointing others to the cross, and preparing for the Lord's return. Living with *purposeful urgency*, we must unapologetically declare Jesus's message of repentance and hope to a great nation in rapid decline.

God alone knows and holds the future. He controls the timing of all things. That is *His* business. But no matter how history plays out in the days to come, may heaven one day say of us, "This was their finest hour!"

Notes

Chapter 1—Is America Really in Decline?

1. See http://www.kwch.com/content/news/Strong-Oklahoma-earthquake-felt-in-Kansas-392239191.html.

2. Isaiah 5:20.

3. See http://www.washingtontimes.com/news/2013/sep/12/4-in10-american-adults-were-living-end-times/.

4. While technically, Egypt still exists as a nation, its once-world-renown glory and prominence as an ancient superpower ended when it was conquered by Alexander the Great in 332 BC.

5. Psalm 46:6.

6. Psalm 46:1.

7. See also Jeremiah 51:25, where Babylon is described as a "destroying mountain" that God will make into a "burnt out mountain."

8. Psalm 144:4; 1 Chronicles 29:15; Job 8:9; James 4:14; Psalm 102:11; 1 Peter 1:24.

9. Daniel 5:1-31.

10. See https://www.barna.com/research/2015-state-of-atheism-in-america/.

11. See https://www.washingtonpost.com/news/acts-of-faith/wp/2015/05/12/christianity-faces-sharp-decline-as-americans-are-becoming-even-less-affiliated-with-religion/.

12. See http://www.cnn.com/2015/06/26/politics/supreme-court-same-sex-marriage-ruling/.

13. Leviticus 18:22; 20:13.

14. Romans 1:26-28; 1 Corinthians 6:9-10.

15. See http://www.bbc.com/future/story/20160623-polyamorous-relationships-may-be-the-future-of-love.

16. See http://www.usnews.com/news/articles/2015/06/29/
     polyamorous-rights-advocates-see-marriage-equality-coming-for-them.

17. See ttp://brennerbrief.com/obama-associates-and-the-north-american-man-boy
     -love-association-nambla/.

18. See http://abcnews.go.com/US/story?id=95942&page=1.

19. See http://www.usatoday.com/story/news/nation/2015/08/16/transgender-
     individuals-face-high-rates—suicide-attempts/31626633/ This statistic is com-
     pared to 4.6 percent of the general population. The LGBT community would argue
     that it's the mistreatment transgenders receive from the public (and presumably the
     Christian community) that contributes to this alarmingly high rate.

20. See http://www.thecollegefix.com/post/23519/.

21. See http://abcnews.go.com/blogs/headlines/2014/02/
     heres-a-list-of-58-gender-options-for-facebook-users/.

22. See https://uwm.edu/lgbtrc/support/gender-pronouns/.

23. See http://www.washingtontimes.com/news/2016/may/18/
     de-blasio-fine-businesses-wrong-gender-pronouns/.

24. See http://www.pewresearch.org/fact-tank/2014/12/22/
     less-than-half-of-u-s-kids-today-live-in-a-traditional-family/.

25. It is not the job of our education system to lead or guide America's children spiritu-
     ally. That is the role of godly parents and the church. To me, taking prayer out of the
     hands of teachers (who comprise people of many faiths, beliefs, and philosophies) is
     prudent. The removal of prayer, however, was nevertheless a gesture symbolic of our
     country's systematic elimination of God from American life.

26. See http://www.washingtontimes.com/news/2014/jan/28/
     whos-godless-now-russia-says-its-us/.

27. John 8:44.

28. John 12:31; 14:30; 16:11.

29. 1 John 5:19.

30. 2 Corinthians 4:4.

31. Ephesians 2:2; 6:12.

32. 2 Corinthians 11:3,14; Ephesians 6:11.

33. Revelation 20:1-3.

34. This is the percentage of scriptures that were prophetic at the time of their writing.

Chapter 2—How Firm a Foundation

1. John Adams, *The Works of John Adams*, Vol. IX, ed. Charles Francis Adams (Boston:
    Little, Brown, 1854), 401.

2. See https://www.monticello.org/site/research-and-collections/mammoth-cheese.

3. Thomas Jefferson to Peter Carr, 10 August 1787, in *Papers of Thomas Jefferson*, Volume 12 (Princeton: Princeton University Press, 1955), 15.

4. See http://www.patheos.com/blogs/anxiousbench/2015/03/woven-into-the-fabric-of-our-country-islam-in-early-america/.

5. See https://history.state.gov/milestones/1801-1829/barbary-war.

6. George Santayana, *The Life of Reason or the Phases of Human Progress: Reason in Common Sense* (New York: Scribner's, 1905), 284.

7. Cf. Deuteronomy 4:9,23; 5:15; 8:1-12,18; 9:7-8; 1 Chronicles 16:12,15.

8. Luke 22:19.

9. Ecclesiastes 12:1; Psalm 119:55; Isaiah 46:9; 2 Peter 3:1; Revelation 2:5.

10. Jeremiah 17:9; Romans 3:10-12,23.

11. This separation arose due to Rome's refusal to grant Henry VIII a marriage annulment from his then-wife Catherine of Aragon. So the king simply broke ties with the Pope and began his own state-sponsored church. Thus the Church of England was born. But though he shut down and destroyed his country's Catholic monasteries and abbeys, confiscating wealth and land, the Catholic Church itself changed very little in its beliefs and practices.

12. See http://www.christianitytoday.com/history/issues/issue-28/1534-act-of-supremacy.html.

13. Henry VIII's *The Act of Six Articles*, passed by the English Parliament in 1539, outlined what became law for English citizens—see http://www.reformationhappens.com/works/6articles/.

14. William Bradford, *Bradford's History of the Plymouth Settlement* (New York: E.P. Dutton, 1920), 21.

15. See http://www.christianity.com/church/church-history/timeline/1701-1800/the-great-awakening-11630212.html.

16. See http://www.increasinglearning.com/franklin-conversion.html for more information regarding Benjamin Franklin's spiritual journey.

17. See http://nationalhumanitiescenter.org/pds/becomingamer/ideas/text2/franklinwhitefield.pdf from Franklin's autobiography.

18. See http://www.archives.gov/exhibits/charters/constitution_transcript.html.

19. See http://libertyunderfire.org/2011/07/five-references-to-god-in-the-declaration-of-independence/.

20. Actually, only one, as Lyman Hall had left the ministry to pursue a medical practice, leaving John Witherspoon as the lone clergy signer. See https://www.archives.gov/exhibits/charters/declaration_signers_gallery_facts.pdf.

21. See http://www.adherents.com/gov/Founding_Fathers_Religion.html.

22. James Hutson, *Religion and the Founding of the American Republic* (Washington, DC: Library of Congress, 1998), 96; quoting from a handwritten history in possession of the Library of Congress, "Washington Parish, Washington City," by Rev. Ethan Allen.

23. See http://connecticutsar.org/the-price-they-paid/.

24. John Adams, *The Works of John Adams, Second President of the United States*, ed. Charles Francis Adams (Boston: Little, Brown, 1856), Vol. X, 45-46. To Thomas Jefferson on June 28, 1813.

25. *Reports of Committees of the House of Representatives Made During the First Session of the Thirty-Third Congress* (Washington, DC: A.O.P. Nicholson, 1854), 6, 8.

26. *Journal of the House of Representatives of the United States: Being the First Session of the Thirty-Fourth Congress* (Washington, DC: Cornelius Wendell, 1855), 354.

27. *Journal of the Senate of the United States of America, Being the Third Session of the Thirty-Seventh Congress* (Washington, DC: Government Printing Office, 1863), 378-379. The full text of the proclamation can be read at http://www.wallbuilders.com/LIBissuesArticles.asp?id=131332.

28. Joseph Story, *Life and Letters of Joseph Story*, ed. William W. Story (Boston: Charles C. Little and James Brown, 1851), Vol. II, 8, 92. Emphasis added.

29. B.F. Morris, *Christian Life and Character of the Civil Institutions of the United States, Developed in the Official and Historical Annals of the Republic* (Philadelphia: George W. Childs, 1864), 639.

30. George Washington, Thanksgiving Proclamation, October 3, 1789.

31. Letter written to John Murray, 1816.

32. See https://www.usa.church/us-history-quotes-about-god-and-the-bible/.

33. David J. Brewer, *The United States: A Christian Nation* (Philadelphia: John C. Winston, 1905), 11, 40, 46.

34. For a more complete and in-depth survey of America's Christian roots, visit http://www.wallbuilders.com.

35. Will Durant, *The Lessons of History* (New York: Simon & Schuster, 1968), 43, 50-51.

Chapter 3—Lessons from an Ancient People

1. See http://winthropsociety.com/doc_charity.php.

2. Ibid.

3. Formally known as postmillennialism, this view of eschatology believes that over an unspecified period of time, the church will help bring about righteousness and peace in the world, followed up by the second coming of Jesus. This belief gained some support in the nineteenth century but quickly declined in the wake of the first World War, when clearly, the world did not get better.

4. The differences and distinctions between Israel and the church are many.

Israel	**Church**
A nation	A bride
Born into by race	Born into by faith
Began with Abraham	Began with Pentecost
Revealed, visible	Hidden, a mystery
Distinct from Gentiles	Includes Jews and Gentiles
God dwelt with Israel	God dwells within believers
Old Covenant	New Covenant
Physical circumcision by man	Spiritual circumcision by Christ

5. An amped-up version of this is called Dominion Theology, or sometimes referred to as "Reconstructionism." This view teaches that it is a Christian's divine duty and right to have dominion over the earth, socially, economically, and politically. This theocratic ideology believes that this dominion by believers over the world will usher in the return of Christ. While it's true that Adam was originally given dominion over the earth and the animal kingdom, that dominion was partially forfeited by sin in the Fall and will not be fully restored until Christ reigns in His millennial kingdom. See Genesis 1:28; Psalm 8:3-9; Daniel 7:27; Revelation 2:26-28; 5:9-10. Clearly we are living in a time of temporary satanic dominion on earth (Luke 4:5-8; 1 John 5:19; 2 Corinthians 4:4; Ephesians 2:2; 6:12).

6. See http://www.space.com/17262-quasar-definition.html.

7. 1 Peter 3:20.

8. Genesis 17:5. *Abram* means "exalted father," and *Abraham* means "father of a great multitude."

9. See Joshua 24:2. The great Ziggurat of Ur, built around 2100 BC, was dedicated to this god. Eroded over time, a partially reconstructed version of it can be seen in south Iraq today. Later, prior to their entrance to the Promised Land, the Lord warned Israel regarding worship of the constellations, a sin punishable by death (Deuteronomy 4:19; 17:2-5). Under wicked kings, this command was ignored (see 2 Kings 23:5-12).

10. This covenant was further restated and reaffirmed in Genesis 15: 1-7,18-21 and Genesis 17:1-21.

11. Acts 7:2-4. See also Genesis 15:7; Nehemiah 9:7.

12. See Genesis 13:14-15; 15:18-21.

13. Genesis 15:8.

14. With the exception of the birds (Genesis 15:10).

15. Genesis 15:1,13-21.

16. Exodus 3:4; 13:21-22; 19:18; 1 Kings 8:10-12; 18:38.

17. See Jeremiah 34:18-19.

18. Genesis 50:24; Exodus 2:24; Deuteronomy 9:5-6; 2 Kings 13:23; Micah 7:18,20; Malachi 3:6; Luke 1:67-75; Acts 3:25-26.

19. Genesis 17:5. *Abram* means "exalted father," and Abraham means "father of a great multitude" or "father of many nations."

20. Genesis 13:15; 17:7-8,13, 19; 1 Chronicles 16:16-17; Psalm 105:9-10; Jeremiah 31:35-36.

21. Ezekiel 37:21-28; Micah 2:12-13; Jeremiah 23:5-6; Isaiah 61:1-62; 65:17-24; Acts 15:14-17; Revelation 20:4-6.

22. Jesus prophesied this in Matthew 24:1-2.

23. See http://www.jewishvirtuallibrary.org/jsource/Judaism/jewpop.html.

24. See Genesis 20:2-18; 21:22-34; 23:1-20.

25. See http://www.reformjudaismmag.net/rjmag-90s/998sam.html.

26. See https://www.youtube.com/watch?v=yWwyCgUFaJ0.

27. Genesis 12:3; 18:18; 22:18; 26:4; 28:14; Psalm 72:17; Matthew 1:1; Luke 3:34; Acts 3:25; Galatians 3:8,16.

28. Revelation 7:9.

29. 1 Corinthians 10:32.

30. Romans 16:25; Ephesians 3:3-10; Ephesians 5:32.

31. Romans 11:17,19.

32. Romans 11:29.

33. Genesis 19:1-29; Jonah 1:1-2, though Nineveh's wickedness was great and scheduled for judgment, it was spared after Jonah's preaching. However, 100 years later, the Ninevites had returned to their heathen ways. God sent the prophet Nahum, calling them to repentance and threatening judgment and destruction if they refused. True to His word, Nineveh was destroyed in 612 BC by the Medes, marking the end of the Assyrian Empire. And as prophesied by Nahum in 3:11, the city was "hidden." In fact, it was hidden for some 2400 years before being rediscovered in 1847 by British archeologist Austen Henry Layard.

34. Genesis 6:5-7; Isaiah 34:5; 66:1-5; Psalm 110:6; Matthew 25:32.

35. Daniel 4:28-37; Acts 12:23.

36. Isaiah 47:6-11 NIV.

37. Ezekiel 5:15; Jeremiah 25:7-11.

Chapter 4—The Road to Abandonment

1. John 1:1-3.

2. John 17:3.

3. See http://www.albertmohler.com/2016/01/20/
the-scandal-of-biblical-illiteracy-its-our-problem-4/.

4. Ibid.

5. Ibid.

6. See http://www.christianitytoday.com/edstetzer/2014/october/biblical-illiteracy-by-numbers.html.

7. Romans 8:3; 2 Corinthians 5:21; 1 John 2:2.

8. Matthew 27:46.

9. Romans 6:23.

10. John 3:16,36; Romans 9:22; 1 Corinthians 16:22; Ephesians 2:3; 5:6.

11. As those whose sins have been removed by Christ's death, we will never have to pay for our sins in eternity. Jesus paid it all. However, that does not exempt us from reaping the natural consequences of sin in this life. Further, though God does not punish His children with wrath, He does discipline every one of us "for our good, that we may (experientially) share in His holiness." Not all of this discipline is due to sin; some of it is simply part of our training in righteousness. See Hebrews 12:3-11.

12. Matthew 28:18-20; John 6:37-39; 10:27-29; Romans 8:33-39; 2 Timothy 2:13; Hebrews 13:5.

13. Galatians 1:11-12, 17-18; 2 Peter 1:20-21.

14. Romans 2:14-15; Psalm 19:1-6.

15. 1 Timothy 4:2.

16. Psalm 8; 89:11.

17. C.S. Lewis, *The Case for Christianity* (Nashville, TN: Broadman & Holman, 2000), 32.

18. 2 Corinthians 4:4.

19. 2 Peter 3:3-5.

20. Matthew 25:26-30.

21. 2 Thessalonians 2:10-12.

22. The phrase "they became fools" is from a Greek verb whose adjective form means "dull or stupid."

23. See http://www.pewforum.org/2012/12/18/global-religious-landscape-exec/. Of this number, 1.1 billion are "religiously unaffiliated," and yet many of these still profess belief in some deity or "universal spirit."

24. Revelation 9:20; 13:11-18.

25. Acts 17:27.

26. Matthew 5:25; 10:17,19,21; 18:34; Mark 1:14; Acts 8:3.

27. 2 Peter 2:4. These may be the angels who cohabitated with mortal women in Genesis 6:1-3; Jude 6.

28. Romans 4:25; 8:32.

29. Genesis 2:24-25.

30. Jeremiah 17:9.

31. See http://www.techaddiction.ca/files/porn-addiction-statistics.jpg.

32. See http://www.unh.edu/ccrc/pdf/CV169.pdf.

33. See http://www.nbcnews.com/business/business-news/things-are-looking-americas-porn-industry-n289431.

34. See http://www.cdc.gov/std/life-stages-populations/stdfact-msm.htm.

35. Paul uses only two gender references—male and female. Moses and Jesus join him in affirming this, from the moment of creation (Genesis 1:26-27; Matthew 19:4-5). Thus there is no room in human civilization for inventing multiple genders in order to appease the imaginations or inclinations. Doing so only placates our insanity and deepens our gender confusion and perpetuates our love affair with sexual deviance.

36. Psalm 51:5; 58:3; Romans 3:10-12; 23.

37. See http://pulpitandpen.org/2016/10/25/jen-hatmaker-affirms-gay-marriage-proves-she-has-no-idea-who-god-is/.

38. Genesis 19:13-14,24-25; Jude 7.

39. Charles Hodge, *Commentary on the Epistle to the Romans* (Grand Rapids: Eerdmans, 1983), 42.

40. See http://www.livescience.com/50725-same-sex-marriage-history.html.

41. See https://www.brandeis.edu/projects/fse/judaism/docs/essays/same-sex-marriage.pdf.

42. 1 Corinthians 6:9-11; 10:13.

43. Acts 4:12; Romans 10:13.

44. John 1:14,18.

45. Romans 6:1-14.

46. Despite being a small percentage of the American population, male-to-male intercourse accounts for more than half of all new HIV cases and more than 80 percent of syphilis cases. See http://www.cdc.gov/msmhealth/std.htm.

47. See https://carm.org/statistics-homosexual-promiscuity.

48. Psalm 2:5,12; 76:6-7; 78:49-51; 90:7-9; Psalm 81:11-12; Hosea 4:17; Acts 14:6; Revelation 14:11; 20:11-15.

49. Matthew 28:18-20; John 10:27-30; 2 Timothy 2:13; Hebrews 13:5.

50. The Lord temporarily turned away from Israel because of her sin (see Acts 7:38-42).

51. Hebrews 5:14.

52. See Genesis 15:16.

Chapter 5—America's Holocaust

1. See http://www.pewresearch.org/fact-tank/2015/10/06/how-abortion-is-regulated-around-the-world/. Roughly 25 percent of these countries allow abortion only when the mother's life is in danger.

2. Genesis 1:26; Job 10:8-11; Psalm 119:73; 139:13-16; Isaiah 44:24.

3. Romans 12:1.

4. See https://archive.org/stream/cu31924000900849/cu31924000900849_djvu.txt.

5. See https://medlineplus.gov/druginfo/natural/480.html.

6. See http://www.newenglishreview.org/custpage.cfm/frm/123665/sec_id/123665.

7. See http://www.abort73.com/abortion_facts/ancient_abortion_history/.

8. See http://www.abort73.com/abortion_facts/ancient_abortion_history/.

9. See http://www.feminist.com/resources/ourbodies/abortion.html.

10. Some of the remains were determined to be children up to the age of six.

11. L.E. Stager and S.R. Wolff, S.R., "Child Sacrifice at Carthage—Religious Rite or Population Control?", *Biblical Archaeology Review* (Jan/Feb 1984), 45.

12. Plutarch, *De superstitione* 171, The Loeb Classical Library.

13. See http://www.biblearchaeology.org/post/2012/01/05/Abortion-and-the-Ancient-Practice-of-Child-Sacrifice.aspx#Article.

14. 1 Kings 11:31-33.

15. 1 Kings 11:7, referred to as "Tophet" in Jeremiah 7:30-34, and the "Mount of Corruption" in 2 Kings 23:13.

16. Jeremiah 7:32.

17. See http://www.theopedia.com/gehenna.

18. 2 Kings 23:10; Matthew 10:28; 23:23; Mark 9:43, 45.

19. Romans 12:1-2; 2 Corinthians 6:14-18; Hebrews 6:1-6; 1 Peter 1:14; 4:1-5.

20. Mark Felix, Christian lawyer, Octavius chapter 30.

21. *A Plea for the Christians* 35, Embassy, Chapter 5.

22. AD 250 Letter of Diognetus ch.5, vs.6, http://www.ccel.org/ccel/richardson/fathers.x.i.ii.html.

23. See http://www.orthodox.net/gleanings/abortion.html.

24. See https://www.plannedparenthood.org/learn/abortion.

25. See http://depts.washington.edu/uwcoe/healthtopics/familyplan/term_facts.html.

26. See http://www.johnstonsarchive.net/policy/abortion/abreasons.html.

27. See http://www.washingtontimes.com/news/2016/apr/3/hillary-clinton-unborn-person-has-no-constitutiona/.

28. Used with permission from Dr. Norman Geisler, and taken from original class notes. Though the majority of answers are direct quotes, in some places I summarized for brevity and clarity.

29. See http://www.abort73.com/abortion_facts/ancient_abortion_history/. Other texts attributed to Hippocrates indicate abortion was allowed in certain cases, including specific instructions on how to expel a developing baby.

30. See http://www.prochoice.com/abort_how.html.

31. See http://www.abortionfacts.com/learn-inc/summary-of-abortion-methods.

32. See http://www.weeklystandard.com/dnc-speaker-shouts-her-abortion-and-the-crowd-cheers/article/2003531.

33. See http://abort73.com/abortion_facts/us_abortion_statistics.

34. See "Media Hides Fact" http://www.lifenews.com/2012/09/05/media-hides-fact-planned-parenthood-does-40-of-abortions/.

35. John 8:40,44-45.

36. Revelation 6:10-11.

37. Proverbs 6:16-17.

Chapter 6—Gog, Magog, and 'Merica

1. Franklin Graham, as cited in Troy Anderson, "Where Will America Be at the End of Time?, http://www.charismamag.com/spirit/prophecy/15873-america-at-the-end.

2. Tim LaHaye, "Is the United States in Bible Prophecy?" *National Liberty Journal,* 26:2 (February 1997), 16.

3. God's sovereign hand superintends all of history, but end-times prophecy speaks only to certain events, nations, and individuals.

4. Romans 11:25.

5. Ezekiel 38:1-6. This is a coalition of nations that will come together under the leadership of Gog, prince of Rosh, to invade and destroy tiny Israel. They will be unsuccessful, as God will fight for her (see Ezekiel 38:19-22).

6. The four kingdom symbols can be best understood by the context of Daniel's book and the previous parallel dream of Nebuchadnezzar in Daniel 2. The four kingdoms are Babylon (lion), Medo-Persia (bear, cf. Daniel 8:8,21-22), Greece (leopard), and Rome (fourth beast). This fourth beast will rule the world, and its "ten horns" are explained in Daniel 7:24 as ten kings (a future revival of the Roman Empire) with another "little horn" (7:8) who will subdue 3 of them on his way to world domination as the Antichrist (7:24-25). See also Daniel 11:36-38; 2 Thessalonians 2:3-8; Revelation 13:5-6.

7. Daniel 4:17,34-37.

8. Revelation 12:12.

9. See Exodus 19:4; Deuteronomy 32:11.

10. Ethiopia was later crushed by Assyria in 701 BC.

11. See https://www.raptureready.com/featured/ice/AmericaInBibleProphecy
.html#_ednref5.

12. See http://www.breakingisraelnews.com/64273/
purim-warning-its-time-jews-get-out-america-jewish-world/.

13. See http://www.pre-trib.org/articles/view/is-america-in-bible-prophecy#_edn1.
Emphasis added.

14. Revelation 6:15.

15. 2 Peter 3:1-10.

16. Psalm 2:1-12; Isaiah 34:2-3; Jeremiah 30:11; 46:28; Revelation 10:11; 11:18; 12:5;
14:8; 15:4; 16:19; 17:15; 18:3,23; 19:15.

17. See http://www.usdebtclock.org.

18. See http://www.forbes.com/sites/merrillmatthews/2014/07/02/weve-crossed-the-
tipping-point-most-americans-now-receive-government-benefits/#3dfd80eb6233.

19. See http://www.forbes.com/sites/johntamny/2014/03/09/
the-fed-is-not-printing-money-its-doing-something-much-worse/#1f63024f43a1.

20. See http://christinprophecy.org/articles/the-united-states-in-bible-prophecy/.

21. John 8:44.

22. See https://homeland.house.gov/wp-content/uploads/2015/12/December-Terror-
Threat-Snapshot.pdf.

23. See http://www.military.com/video/operations-and-strategy/domestic-terrorism/
terrorist-training-camps-in-the-us/660940716001.

Chapter 7—The Coming Persecution

1. Martin Luther, *The Complete Sermons of Martin Luther*, Vol. V (Grand Rapids:
Baker, 2000), 41.

2. See http://www.cnn.com/2016/01/17/world/christian-persecution-2015/.

3. See https://www.christianhistoryinstitute.org/magazine/article/
start-seeing-persecution/.

4. See http://www.reuters.com/article/
us-religion-christianity-persecution-idUSBRE9070TB20130108.

5. See http://www.cnsnews.com/news/article/lauretta-brown/9-10-worst-countries-
persecution-christians-have-50-or-greater-muslim.

6. See http://www.persecution.org/persecutionnl/201701/ICC%202016%20Hall%20
of%20Shame%20Report.pdf.

7. 1 Kings 18:13.

8. Jeremiah 15:15; 17:18; 20:11; 26:11; 37:15-16; 38:4-6.

9. Daniel 3:13-20; 6:1-20.

10. Esther 3:1-12; 5:14.

11. Hebrews 11:35-38.

12. See also Matthew 10:22; Mark 13:11-13; Luke 21:12-16.

13. Revelation 17:6.

14. Proverbs 16:2; Jeremiah 17:10; 1 Corinthians 4:5; Hebrews 4:12-13.

15. 2 Corinthians 2:15-16.

16. 1 Corinthians 1:18.

17. Jeremiah 17:9; Romans 12:2; 2 Corinthians 4:4.

18. 1 John 3:13.

19. In Scripture, the term "last days" refers to the period of time between Paul's present day and the Lord's return for His bride. There is every indication that as that time draws near, like birth pangs, evil will intensify (1 Timothy 4:1-5).

20. 2 Timothy 3:1-9.

21. Colossians 1:24; see also 2 Corinthians 1:5; 11:23-28 Galatians 6:17.

22. Acts 9:4.

23. Revelation 6:15-17; 16:9, 11,21.

24. See https://www.statista.com/statistics/264810/number-of-monthly-active-facebook-users-worldwide/.

25. Psalm 34:13; Proverbs 12:18; 15:1; 17:28; 21:23; Ephesians 4:29; James 1:26; 3:2-10.

26. Matthew 26:63; 1 Peter 2:23.

27. Philippians 2:15.

28. Matthew 10:34-42.

29. Mark 13:12-13. The time Jesus referred to is the Tribulation period, a time when, unbelievably, unfeigned loyalty to Antichrist will overshadow even familial ties.

30. http://www.pewresearch.org/fact-tank/2016/07/22/muslims-and-islam-key-findings-in-the-u-s-and-around-the-world/.

31. Ibid.

32. An Arabic phrase meaning "God is greater."

33. The word *apostasy* means to "fall away from the faith." To better understand how this is currently happening in American Christianity, see Mark Hitchcock and Jeff Kinley, *The Coming Apostasy, Exposing the Sabotage of Christianity from Within* (Carol Stream, IL: Tyndale, 2017).

34. Revelation 2:4-5. Jesus warned that unless the church at Ephesus repented, He would remove His presence and their influence for the gospel.

35. See http://www.breitbart.com/big-government/2016/06/14/
    aclu-attorney-blames-christians-for-orlando-jihad-attack/.

36. Hebrews 5:14.

37. John 6:2,10-11.

38. Matthew 26:69-75.

39. Romans 8:16.

40. Acts 4:20; 5:29.

Chapter 8—When the Levee Breaks

1. Adrian Rogers, "Has God Removed His Hedge?" Love Worth Finding Ministries with Adrian Rogers, https://www.lwf.org/bible-study/posts/
   has-god-removed-his-hedge-12583.

2. See http://www.npr.org/templates/story/story.php?storyId=5063796.

3. Revelation 13:1; 17:15; see also Daniel 7:2-3.

4. Daniel 7:8; 2 Thessalonians 2:3; Revelation 13:11; Daniel 9:26.

5. 1 John 2:18; 22; 4:3; 2 John 1:7.

6. 1 John 1:18; 2 Thessalonians 2:7.

7. Romans 3:25; Hebrews 2:17; 1 John 2:2.

8. Robert L. Thomas, *Revelation 8-22: An Exegetical Commentary* (Chicago, Moody,
   1995), 54.

9. 2 Thessalonians 2:2—the phrase "day of the Lord" in this context refers to both the
   judgments and the conclusion of the Tribulation period, which also encompasses
   Antichrist's revealing, rise to power, and ultimate defeat at the hands of Jesus at His
   second coming.

10. John 14:26; 15:26; 16:13-14.

11. Genesis 6:3; 20:6; 1 Peter 3:18-20; 2 Peter 2:5; Jude 14-15.

12. John 16:7-11.

13. For a more in-depth study into why some doubt the reality of the rapture, and why
    I defend it, see my book *Wake the Bride: Facing These Last Days with Your Eyes Wide
    Open* (Eugene, OR: Harvest House, 2015).

14. 1 Thessalonians 4:13-18; John 14:1-3.

15. Psalm 139:7-10.

16. John 3:8; Ecclesiastes 11:5; Psalm 115:3; 135:6.

17. J. Dwight Pentecost, *Things to Come: A Study in Biblical Eschatology* (Grand Rapids:
    Zondervan, 1958), 262.

18. See also 1 Thessalonians 5:2.

19. 1 Corinthians 1:7; 16:22; Philippians 3:20; 4:5; 1 Thessalonians 1:10; Titus 2:13; Hebrews 9:28; 1 Peter 1:13; Jude 1:21; Revelation 3:11; 22:7, 12,17,20.

20. 1 Corinthians 15:51-58; 1 Thessalonians 4:13-18.

21. 1 Thessalonians 4:17.

22. Mark 3:14; John 14:3; 17:6, 24; Ephesians 1:4; Philippians 1:23; 1 Thessalonians 4:17; Revelation 17:14.

23. John 11:43; see also John 5:28.

24. Matthew 25:6.

25. Other angels and another trumpet will be used to gather Tribulation believers in order to usher them into Christ's millennial kingdom at the close of the seven-year period.

26. Exodus 19:16-19; Numbers 10:1-3.

27. 1 Corinthians 15:51-57. No doubt those whose flesh has long since decomposed will mysteriously and supernaturally be re-created into imperishable bodies. This is not a problem for a God, who can speak entire galaxies into existence.

28. Romans 11:25; 16:25; Ephesians 3:3-5,9.

29. Luke 15:7-10.

30. Titus 2:13.

31. Matthew 5:13-15.

32. Psalm 34:8.

33. Ephesians 2:2-3.

34. See Revelation 6:15-17.

35. I detailed how this is currently happening in our country in my book *As It Was in the Days of Noah: Warnings from Bible Prophecy about the Coming Global Storm* (Eugene, OR: Harvest House, 2014).

36. Revelation 12:12.

Chapter 9—How Close Are We?

1. Citing C.S. Lewis, as in Lyle W. Dorsett, *The Essential C.S. Lewis* (New York: Scribner, 1996), 390.

2. 2 Timothy 3:1.

3. See https://www.theburningplatform.com/tag/david-walker/.

4. Genesis 15:16.

5. 1 Chronicles 12:32.

6. Another view often associated with the mid-Trib view is the Pre-Wrath view, which states that believers are raptured at some point during the Tribulation—before

God's wrath begins with the trumpet and bowl judgments, but sometime *after* the seal judgments (which Pre-Wrath advocates see as Satan's wrath).

7. Matthew 5:22,29-30; 7:13-23; 8:10-12; 10:28; 13:49-50; 18:8-9; 19:1-12; 22:11-14; 23:1-36; 24:50-51; 25:29-30, 40-46; Mark 3:28-29; 9:43-48; Luke 10:14-15; 12:4-5; 13:24-28; 16:22-28; John 5:22-29; 14:6.

8. Matthew 7:13-29.

9. John 6:1-2, 16, 44,52-66.

10. Acts 1:7.

11. 1 Thessalonians 4:13.

12. I believe in the rapture for many reasons: including: (1) The pattern of divine rescue from God's wrath in Scripture (Genesis 6-8; 19); (2) the promise of Jesus to return for His disciples (John 14:1-3); (3) the prophecy of Paul (1 Thessalonians 4:13-19); and the portrayal of the church in the book of Revelation (Revelation 4-19). For a more in-depth treatment of this subject, see my book *Wake the Bride: Facing These Last Days with Your Eyes Wide Open* (Eugene, OR: Harvest House, 2015).

13. Jeremiah 30:1-51; Ezekiel 34:11-24; 37; Zechariah 10:6-10.

14. See http://www.cnn.com/2016/05/09/middleeast/russia-military-syria/.

15. Ezekiel 38:1-7 identifies these nations by name, and I have included their modern-day equivalents. They are: Rosh (Russia), Magog (Central Asia/Afghanistan), Meshech (Turkey), Tubal (Turkey), Persia (Iran), Ethiopia (Sudan), Libya (Libya), Gomer (Turkey), and Beth-togarmah (Turkey).

16. Ezekiel 38:16-22.

17. The rapture does not actually begin the Tribulation period, though it does trigger world change and help make conditions ripe for Antichrist's rise to power. In reality, many weeks or months could pass after the rapture before Antichrist's treaty with Israel is signed.

18. Acts 20:28-32; 2 Timothy 3:1-7.

19. See 2 Corinthians 2:17.

20. J. Dwight Pentecost, *Will Man Survive? The Bible Looks at Man's Future* (Grand Rapids: Zondervan, 1971), 58.

21. See http://www.usatoday.com/story/news/world/2014/01/16/wef-biggest-risks-facing-world-2014/4505691/.

22. Revelation 13:16-17.

23. Zechariah 14:4; Acts 1:11; Matthew 24:3.

24. See http://discussions.godandscience.org/viewtopic.php?t=38866.

25. Matthew 16:1-4 NIV.

Chapter 10—A Time for Christians to Rise

1. Matthew 6:10.
2. Hebrews 11:10.
3. Matthew 6:33.
4. Psalm 1:1-6; 16:4; 32:10.
5. John 4:34; 5:19; 6:38.
6. John 17:4; 19:30.
7. Hebrews 12:2.
8. See Philippians 1:21-24.
9. 1 Peter 2:11.
10. Romans 12:1-2; 2 Corinthians 6:14-17.
11. 1 Peter 3:15.
12. Ephesians 4:11-12; 2 Timothy 4:1-5.
13. Revelation 2:4-5; 3:1-3.
14. Revelation 3:1-3.
15. 1 John 4:4; 5:4-5.
16. James 1:22.
17. Matthew 28:19.
18. Revelation 5:9.
19. 1 Timothy 4:1-3; 2 Timothy 3:1-13.
20. See http://www.winstonchurchill.org/resources/speeches/1940-the-finest-hour/122-their-finest-hour.
21. 1 Corinthians 15:58.

Other Harvest House Books

By Jeff Kinley

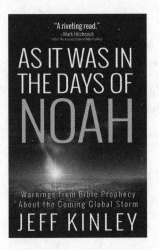

As It Was in the Days of Noah

This powerful book explores the similarities between Noah's day and ours, such as the rapid rise in evil and increasingly flagrant disregard for God. A captivating read that affirms the urgency of living wisely and "redeeming the time" as we see the last days drawing nearer.

Wake the Bride

Many people are unaware of the signs of the times. Many others seem consumed by end-times hype. Kinley's innovative guide to the book of Revelation shows that our primary concern should not be the timing of Christ's return, but rather the spirit and character He desires in His bride.

To learn more about Harvest House books and
to read sample chapters, visit our website:

www.harvesthousepublishers.com

HARVEST HOUSE PUBLISHERS
EUGENE, OREGON